**RECORDED VERSIONS GUITAR**

AUTHENTIC TRANSCRIPTIONS
WITH NOTES AND TABLATURE

# FALL OUT BOY

## FROM UNDER THE CORK TREE

Music transcriptions by Pete Billmann and David Stocker

ISBN 1-4234-40410-6

HAL•LEONARD®
CORPORATION
7777 W. BLUEMOUND RD. P.O. BOX 13819 MILWAUKEE, WI 53213

Visit Hal Leonard Online at
**www.halleonard.com**

# Our Lawyer Made Us Change the Name of This Song So We Wouldn't Get Sued

Words and Music by Patrick Stumph, Peter Wentz, Andrew Hurley and Joseph Trohman

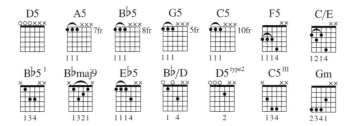

Drop D tuning:
(low to high) D-A-D-G-B-E

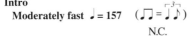

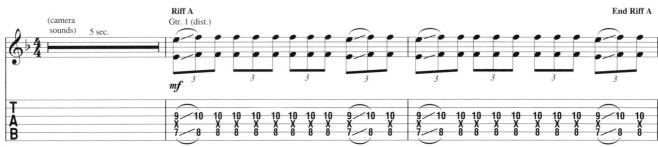

*Composite arrangement
**Chord symbols reflect overall harmony.

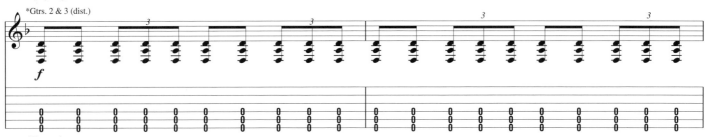

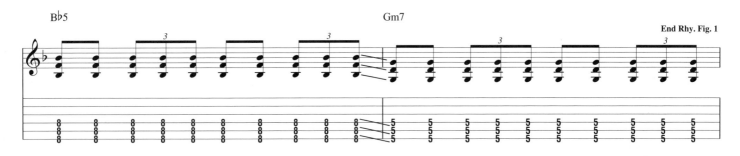

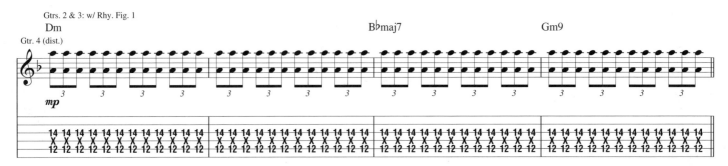

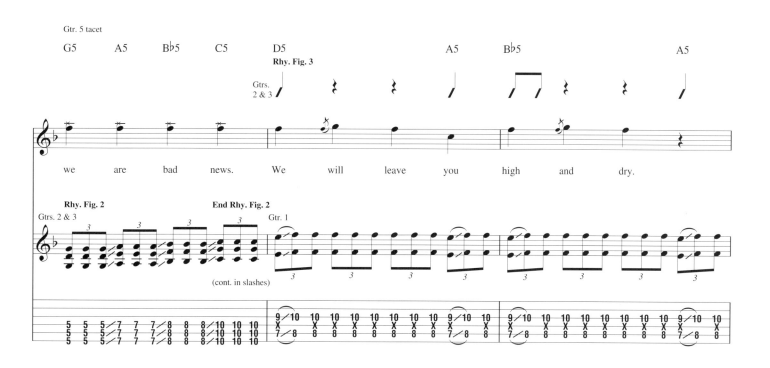

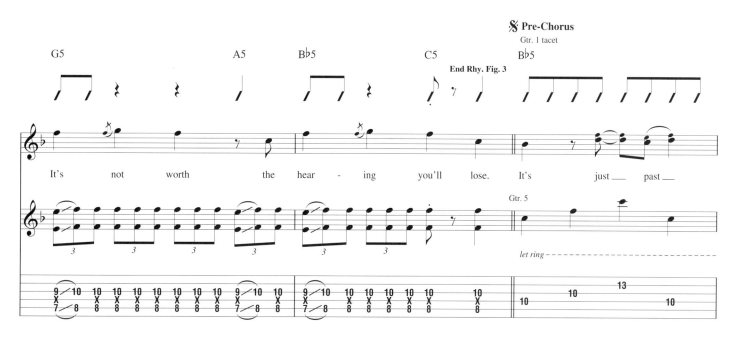

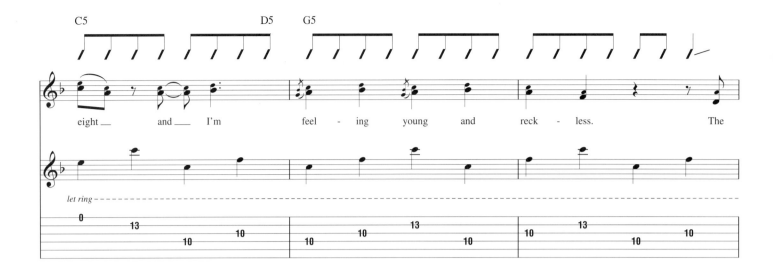

eight ___ and ___ I'm feel - ing young and reck - less. The

rib - bon on ___ my ___ wrist says, "Do not o - pen be - fore Christ - mas." We're

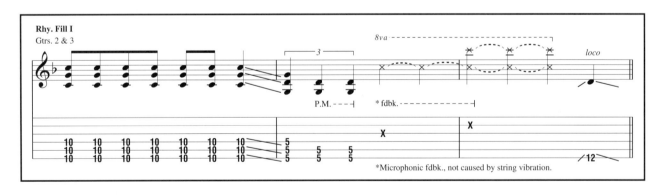

*Microphonic fdbk., not caused by string vibration.

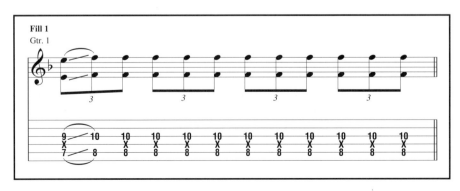

**Chorus**

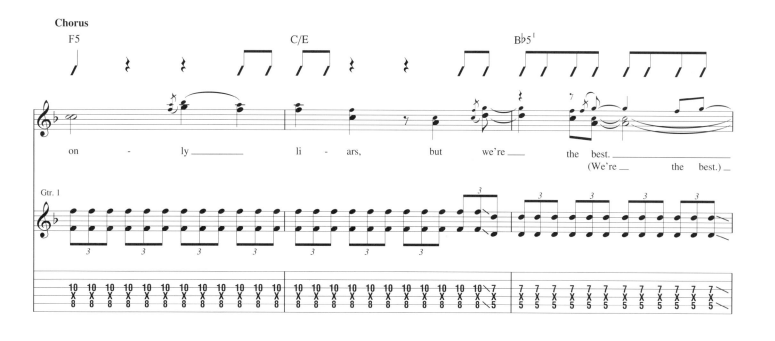

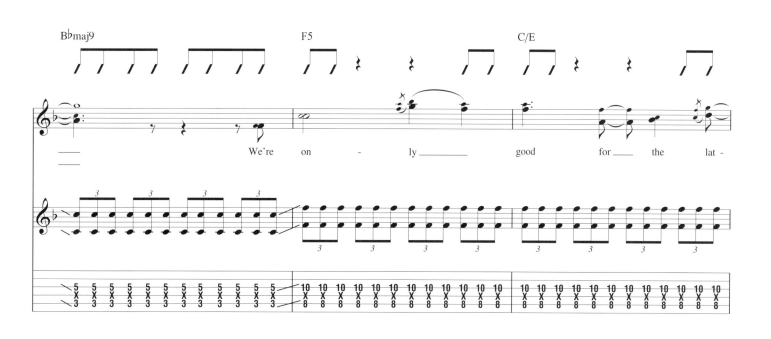

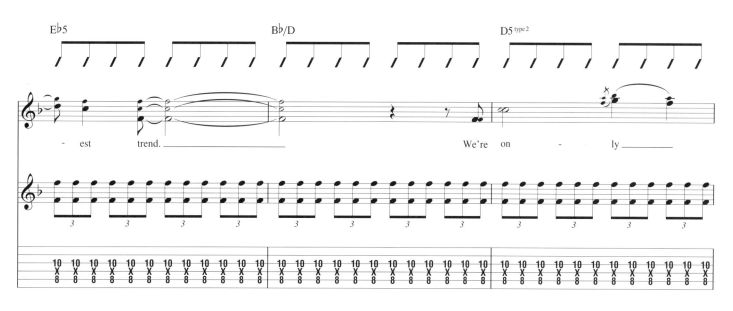

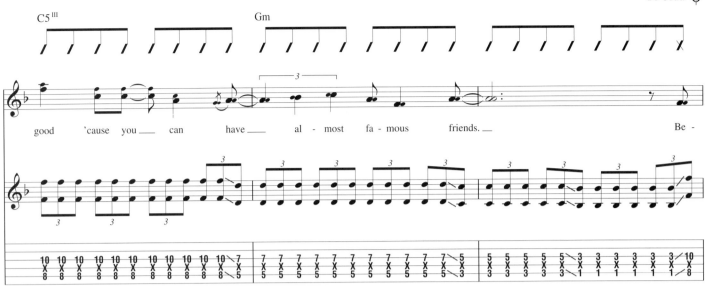

good 'cause you ___ can have ___ al - most fa - mous friends. ___ Be -

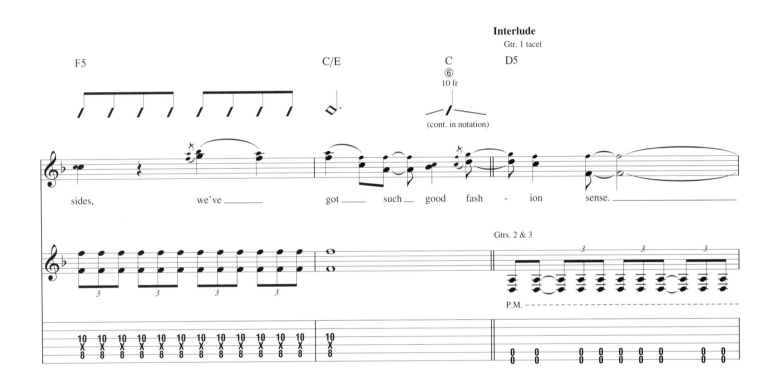

sides, we've ___ got ___ such ___ good fash - ion sense. ___

**Interlude**
Gtr. 1 tacet

Gtrs. 2 & 3

P.M. - - - - - - - - - - - - - - - - - - - - -

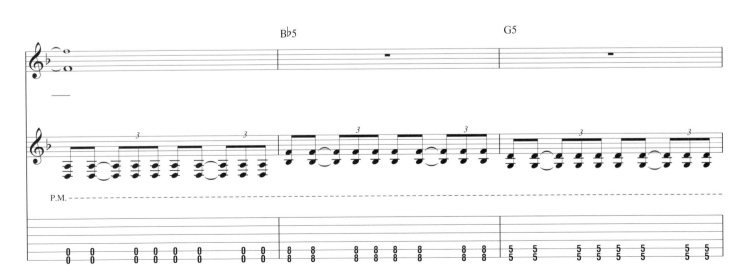

P.M. - - - - - - - - - - - - - - - - - - - - -

Verse

2. Broth-ers and sis-ters, yeah, put these words down

in - to your note-book.
(Spit words like these:)

We're friends when you're

*Gtr. 6: w/ Rhy. Fig. 2

Gtrs. 2 & 3: w/ Rhy. Fig. 3

*Gtr. 6 dist., played *mp*.

**Gtr. 2 to left of slash in tab.

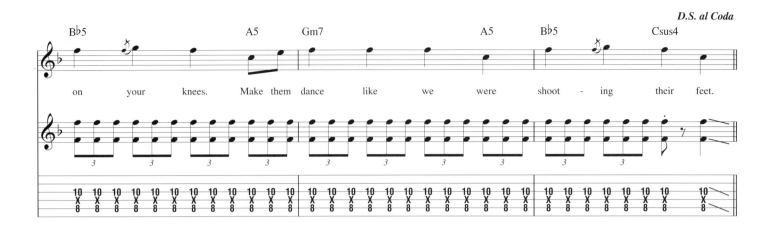

**Coda**

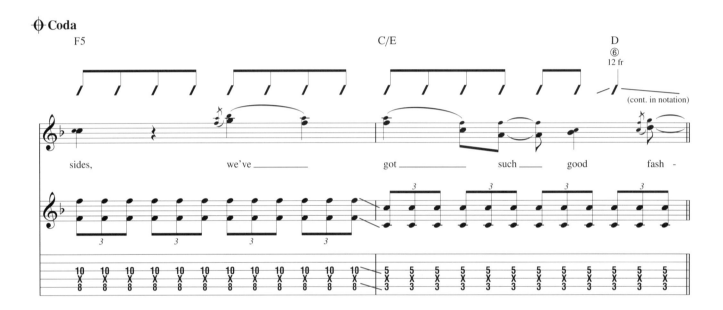

**Interlude**

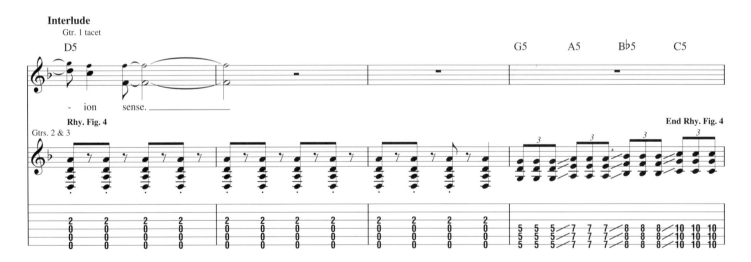

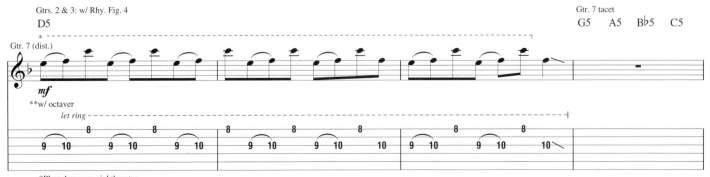

*Played as even eighth-notes.
**Set for one octave below.

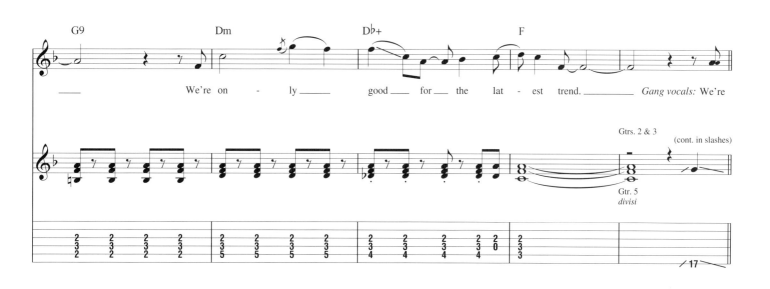

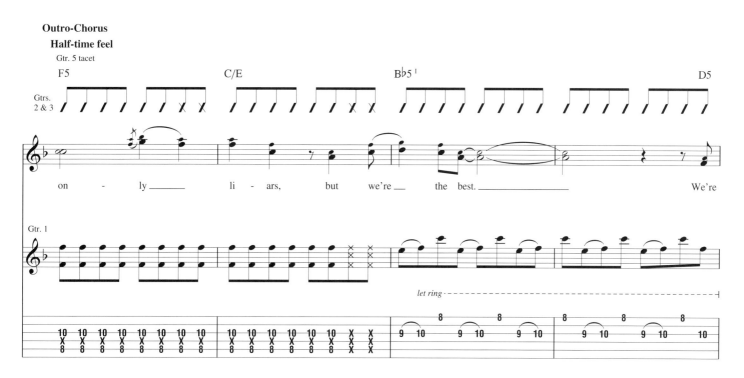

9

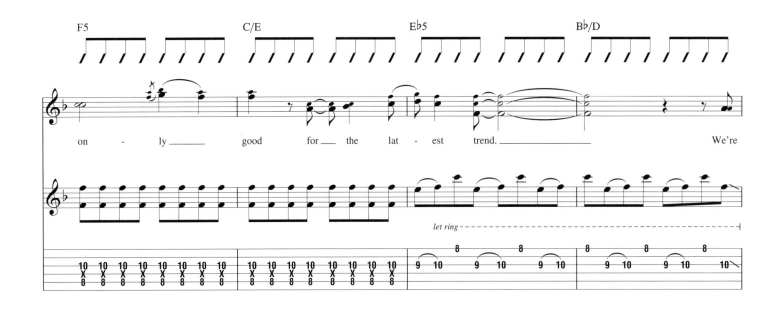

on - ly _____ good for ___ the lat - est trend. _____ We're

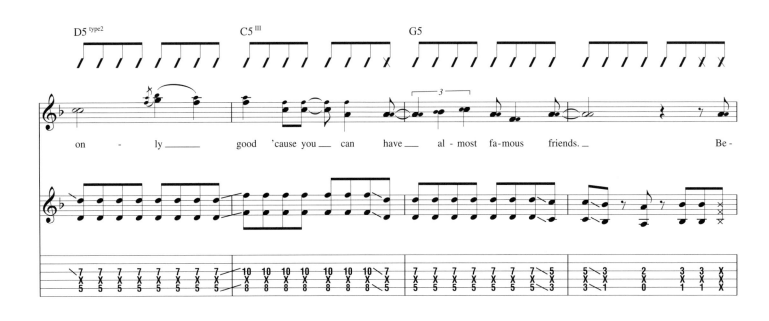

on - ly _____ good 'cause you ___ can have ___ al - most fa - mous friends. ___ Be -

**Free time**

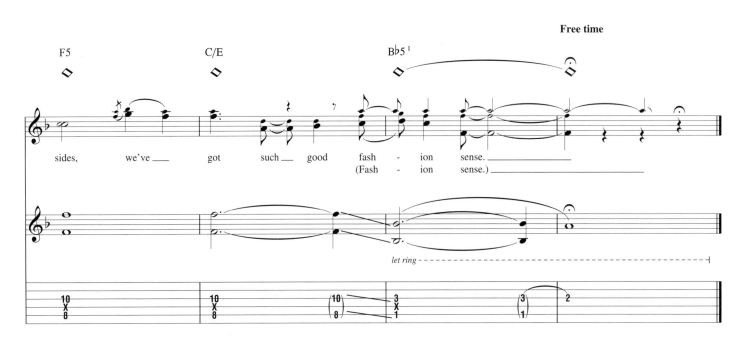

sides, we've ___ got such ___ good fash - ion sense. _____
(Fash - ion sense.) _____

# Of All the Gin Joints in All the World

### Words and Music by Patrick Stumph, Peter Wentz, Andrew Hurley and Joseph Trohman

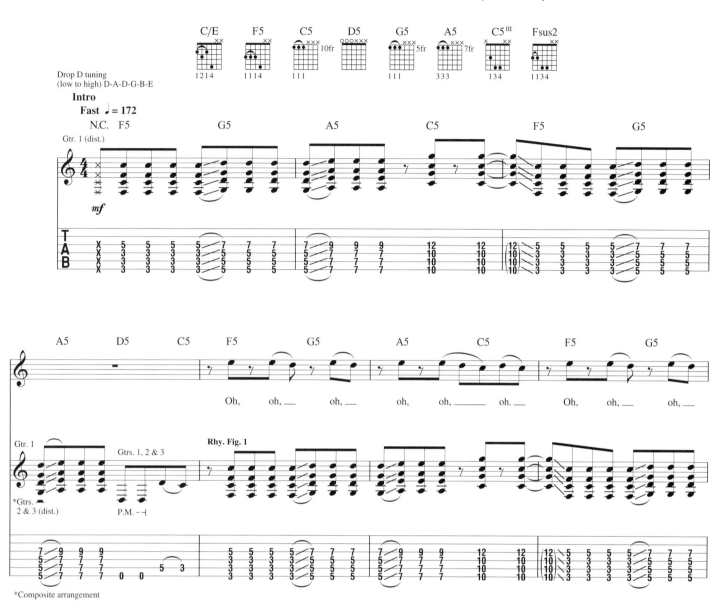

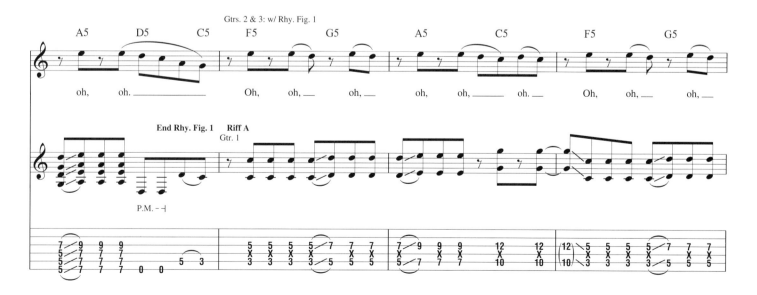

*Composite arrangement

waste my __ time dream - ing of be - ing a - live,... __

...now I on - ly waste it dream-ing of you.

Gtrs. 2 & 3

(cont. in slashes)

P.M. - ⌐

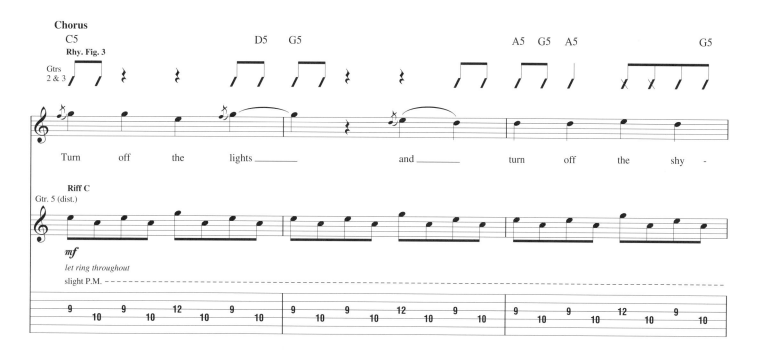

**Chorus**

Rhy. Fig. 3

Gtrs
2 & 3

Turn off the lights __ and __ turn off the shy -

**Riff C**

Gtr. 5 (dist.)

*mf*

*let ring throughout*

slight P.M. - - - - - - - - - - - - - - - - - - - - - - - - - - - - - - - - - - - - - - - -

ness, 'cause all of our moves __ make __

slight P.M. - - - - - - - - - - - - - - - - - - - - - - - - - - - - - - - - - - - - - - - - - - - - - - - - - - - - - - - - - -

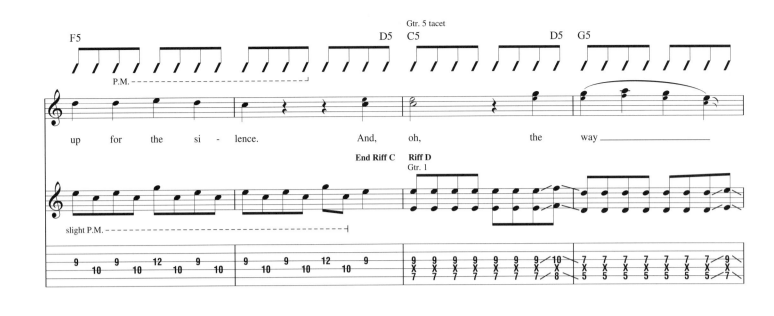

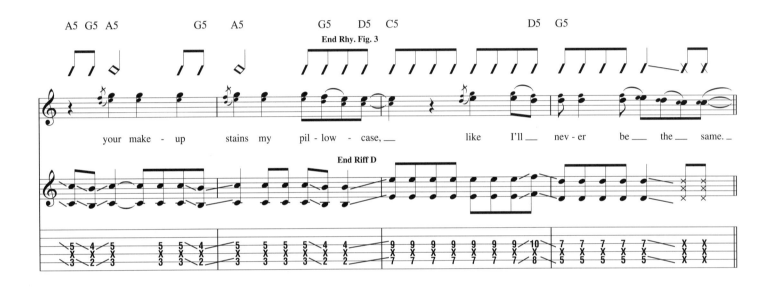

**Interlude**

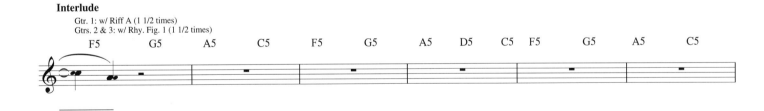

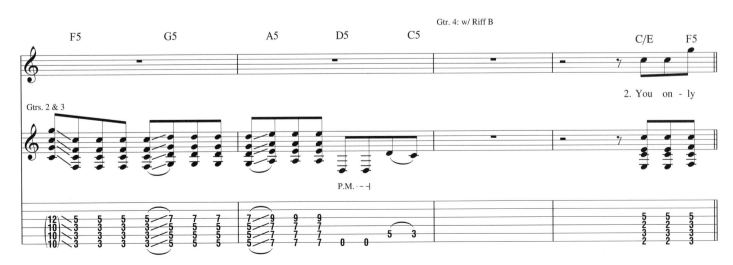

## Verse

hold me up like this      'cause you don't know who I real-ly am.      I used to

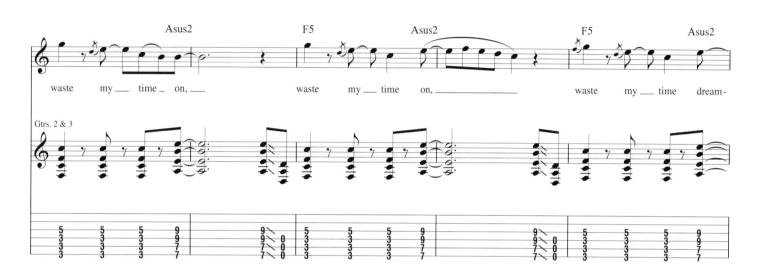

waste my ___ time ___ on, ___     waste my ___ time on, ___     waste my ___ time dream-

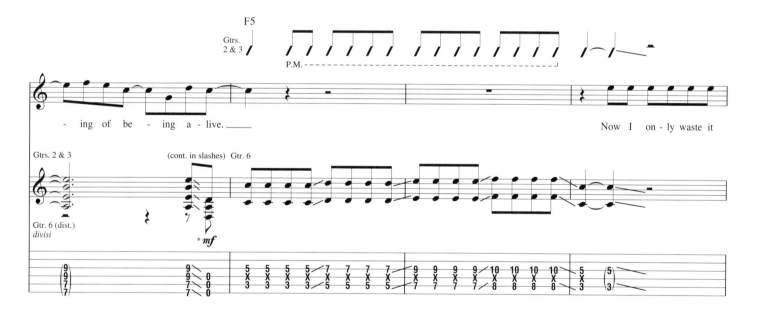

-ing of be - ing a - live. ___     Now I on-ly waste it

## Chorus

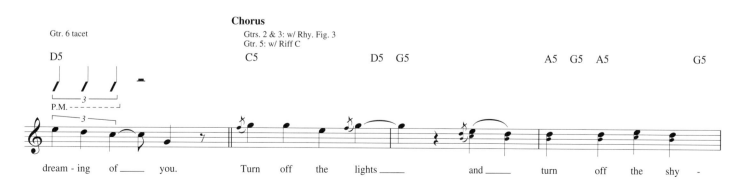

dream - ing of ___ you.     Turn off the lights ___ and ___ turn off the shy -

ness, 'cause all of our moves make up for the si - lence. And,

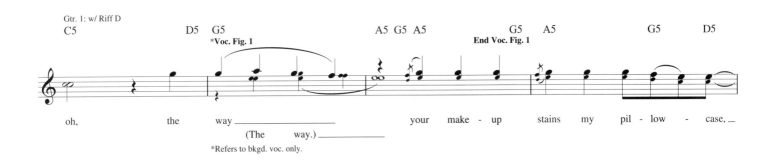

Gtr. 1: w/ Riff D

*Voc. Fig. 1

End Voc. Fig. 1

oh, the way your make - up stains my pil - low - case,

(The way.)

*Refers to bkgd. voc. only.

**Interlude**

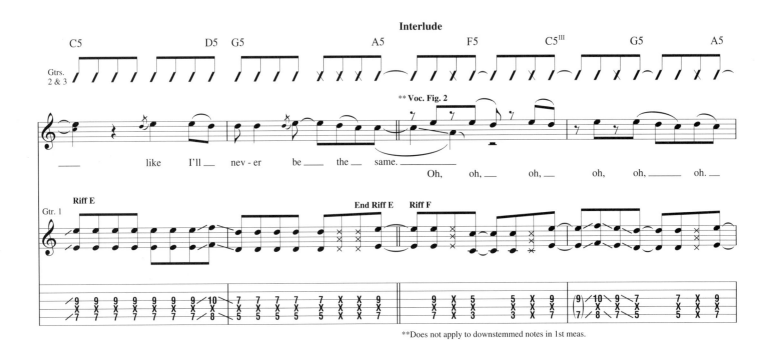

** Voc. Fig. 2

like I'll nev - er be the same. Oh, oh, oh, oh, oh, oh.

Riff E

Gtr. 1

End Riff E    Riff F

**Does not apply to downstemmed notes in 1st meas.

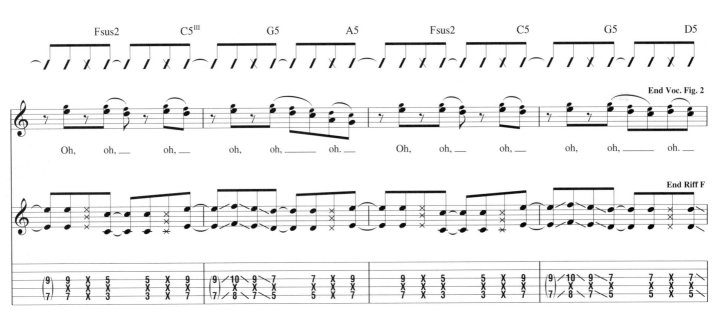

End Voc. Fig. 2

Oh, oh, oh, oh, oh, oh. Oh, oh, oh, oh, oh, oh.

End Riff F

## Chorus

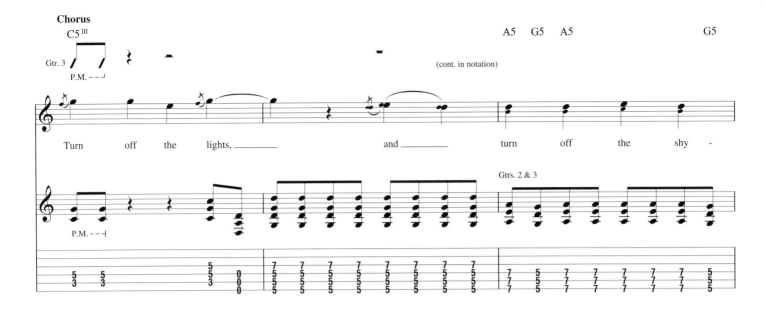

Turn off the lights, _____ and _____ turn off the shy -

ness, 'cause all of our moves _____ make _____

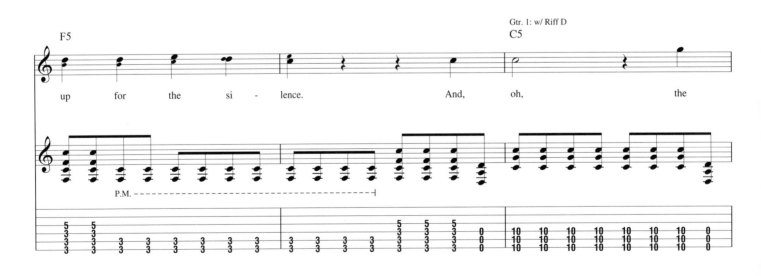

up for the si - lence. And, oh, the

way _____ your make - up stains, _____

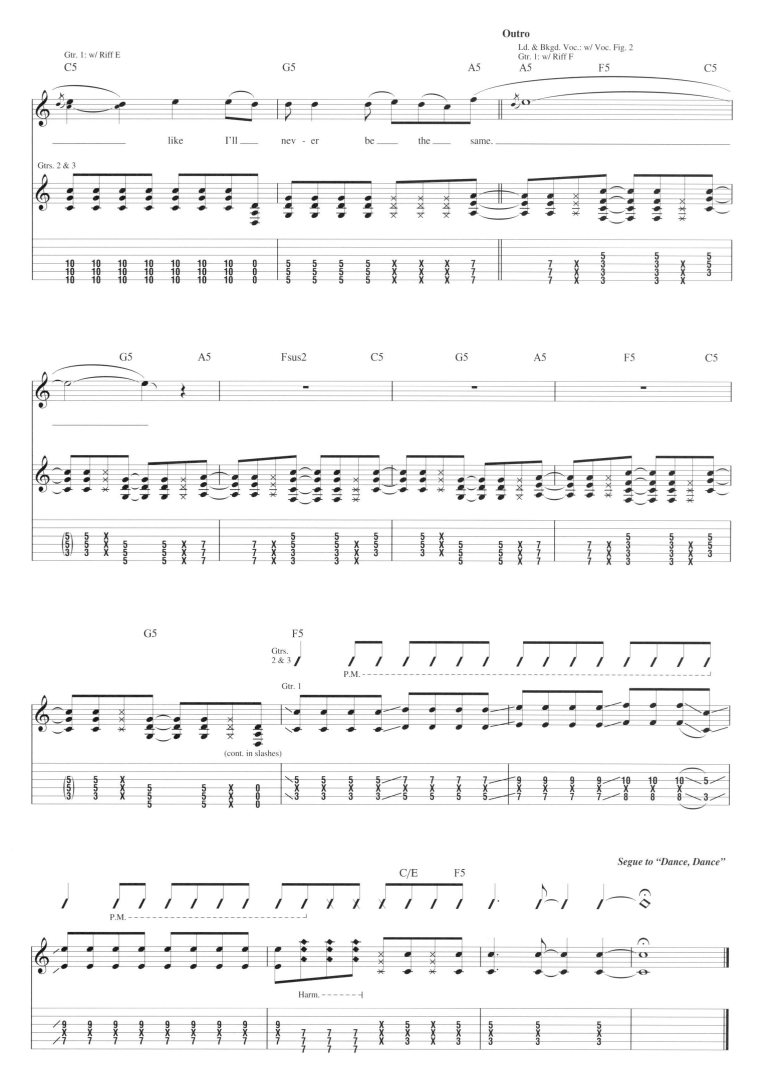

# Dance, Dance

**Words and Music by Patrick Stumph, Peter Wentz, Andrew Hurley and Joseph Trohman**

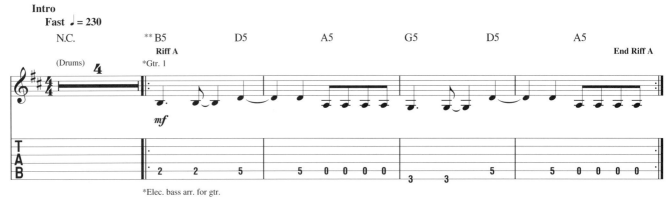

*Elec. bass arr. for gtr.
**Chord symbols reflect implied harmony.

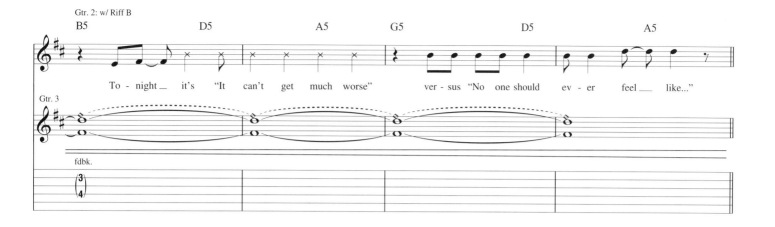

Gtr. 2: w/ Riff B

B5    D5    A5    G5    D5    A5

To - night _ it's "It can't get much worse" ver - sus "No one should ev - er feel _ like..."

Gtr. 3

fdbk.

**Pre-Chorus**

B5  C#5  D5  F#5  E5  F#5  B5    C#5  D5  F#5  E5  F#5  B5

I'm two quar-ters and a heart down, and I don't _ wan-na for-get how your voice sounds. Be-cause words _

Riff C                                                                    End Riff C

*Gtrs. 3 & 4

*Gtr. 3 w/ pick; Gtr. 4 (dist.) Composite arrangement

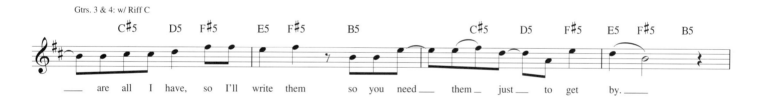

Gtrs. 3 & 4: w/ Riff C

C#5  D5  F#5  E5  F#5  B5    C#5  D5  F#5  E5  F#5  B5

_ are all I have, so I'll write them so you need _ them _ just _ to get by. _

**Chorus**

Bsus2                                  Bm    Bm

Rhy. Fig. 1A

**Gtr. 5

mp

Dance,

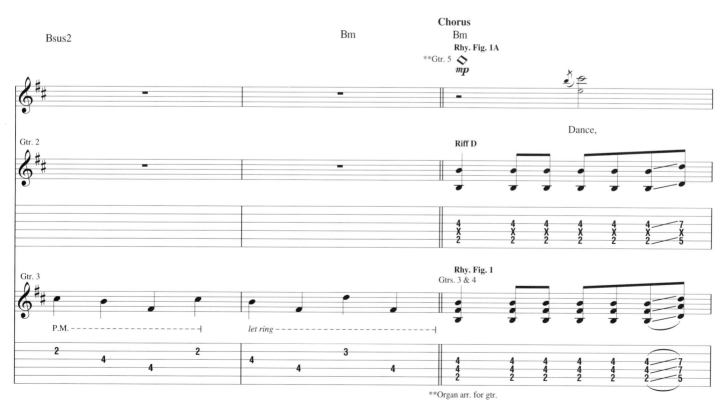

Gtr. 2

Riff D

Gtr. 3

Rhy. Fig. 1
Gtrs. 3 & 4

P.M.                         let ring

**Organ arr. for gtr.

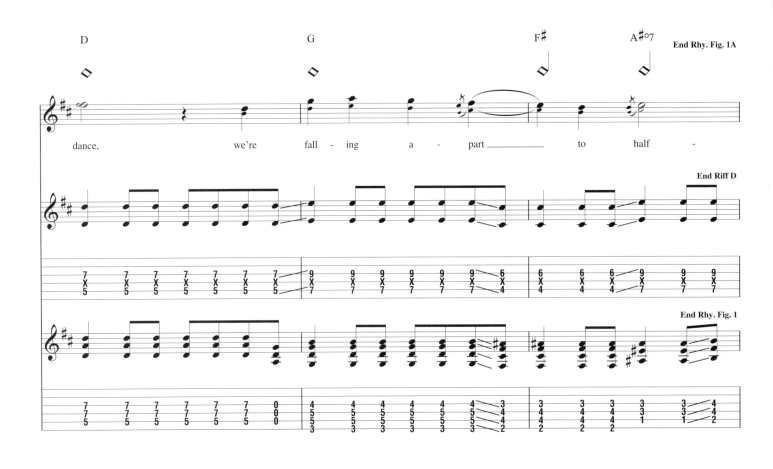

dance, we're fall - ing a - part _____ to half -

Gtr. 2: w/ Riff D (3 times)
Gtrs. 3 & 4: w/ Rhy. Fig. 1 (2 times)
Gtr. 5: w/ Rhy. Fig. 1A (3 times)

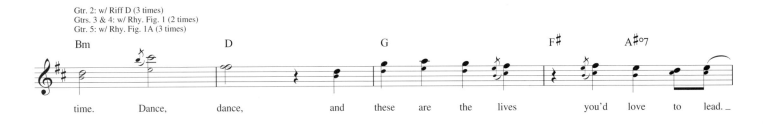

time. Dance, dance, and these are the lives you'd love to lead.

_____ Dance. This is the way they'd _____ love if they knew

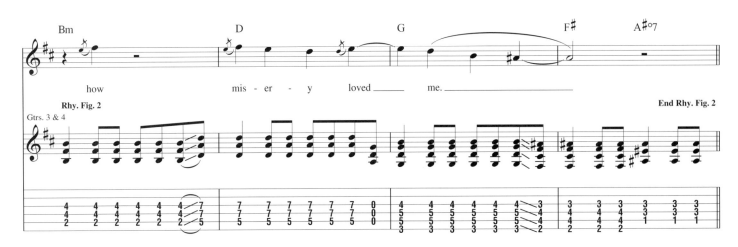

how mis - er - y loved _____ me.

**Interlude**

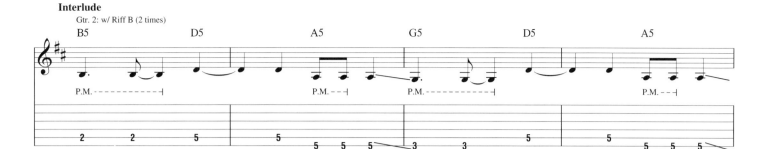

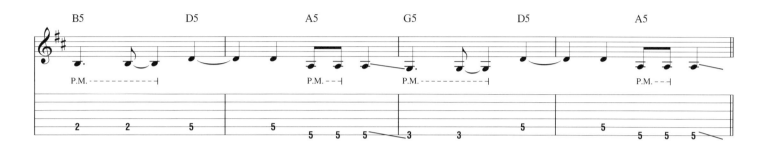

**Verse**

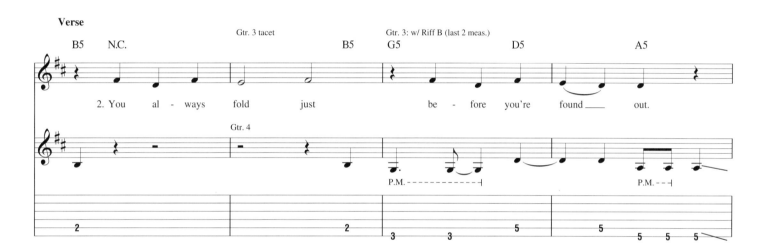

2. You al - ways fold just be - fore you're found ____ out.

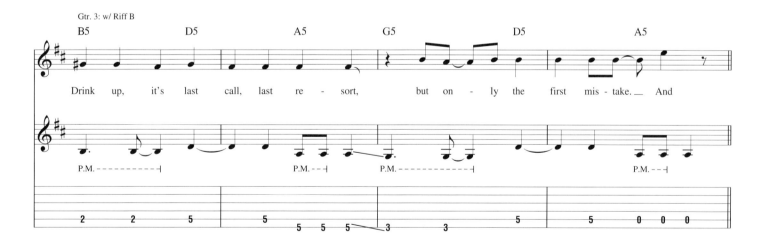

Drink up, it's last call, last re - sort, but on - ly the first mis - take. ____ And

**Pre-Chorus**

I'm two quar - ters and a heart down, and I don't ____ wan - na for - get how your voice sounds. Be - cause words ____

are all I have, so I'll write them so you need _____ them _____ just _____ to get by. _____

**Half-time feel**

Gtr. 1: w/ Riff A

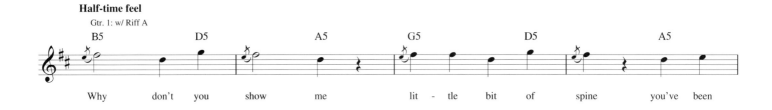

Why don't you show me lit - tle bit of spine you've been

**End half-time feel**

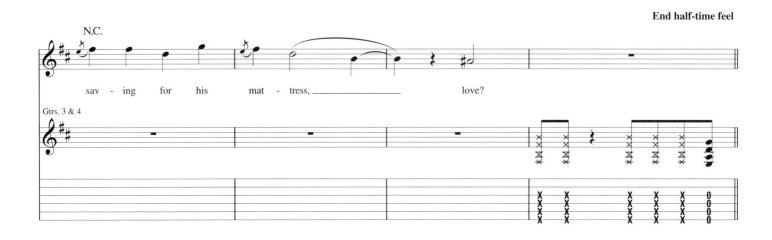

sav - ing for his mat - tress, _____ love?

Gtrs. 3 & 4

**Chorus**

Gtr. 2: w/ Riff D (4 times)
Gtrs. 3 & 4: w/ Rhy. Fig. 1 (4 times)
Gtr. 5: w/ Rhy. Fig. 1A (4 times)

Dance, dance, we're fall - ing a - part _____ to half -

time. Dance, dance, and these are the lives you'd love to lead. _

_____ Dance. This is the way _____ they'd _____ love if they knew

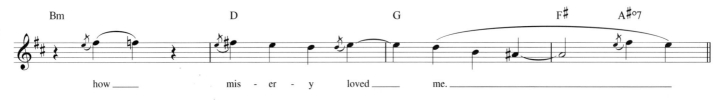

how _____ mis - er - y loved _____ me. _____

**Interlude**

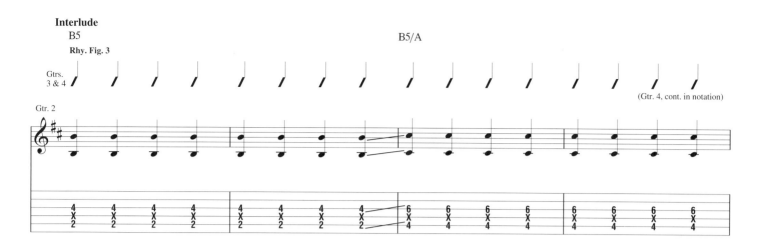

**Bridge**
**Quarter-time feel**

Gtrs. 3 & 4: w/ Rhy. Fig. 3

Why    don't    you    show    me    the    lit - tle    bit    of    spine    you've    been

25

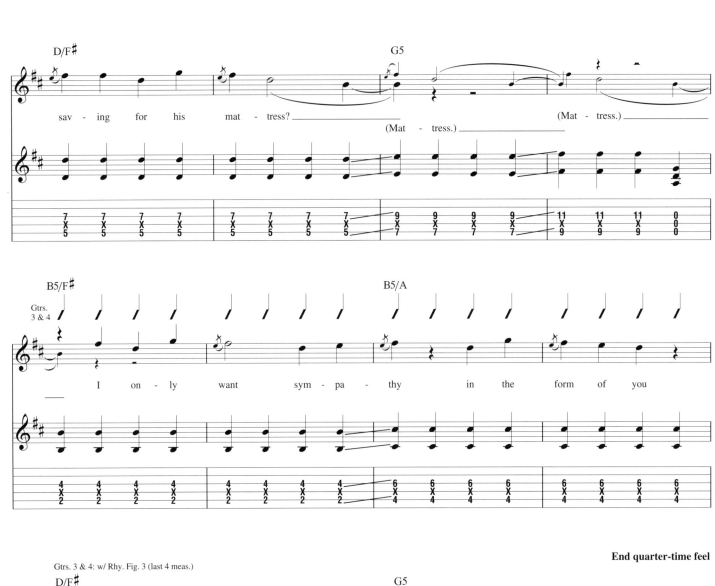

End quarter-time feel

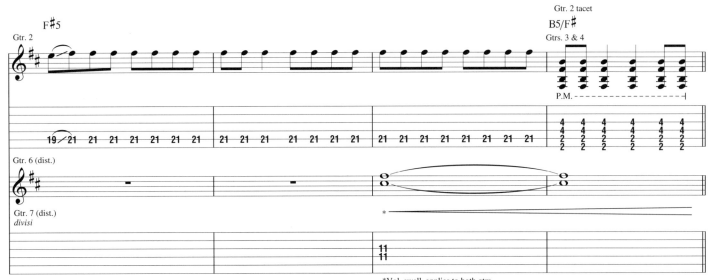

*Vol. swell, applies to both gtrs.

**Chorus**

Gtr. 2: w/ Riff D (6 times)
Gtrs. 3 & 4: w/ Rhy. Fig. 1 (5 times)
Gtr. 5: w/ Rhy. Fig. 1A (6 times)
Gtrs. 6 & 7 tacet

Dance, dance, we're fall - ing a - part _____ to half -

time. Dance, dance, and these are the lives you'd love to lead. _

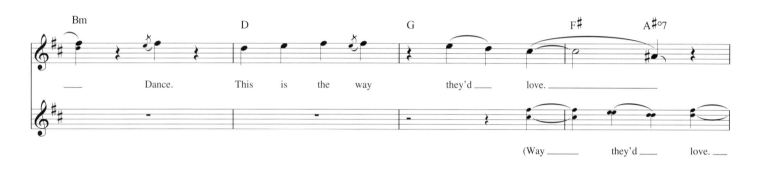

_____ Dance. This is the way they'd _____ love.

(Way _____ they'd _____ love. ___

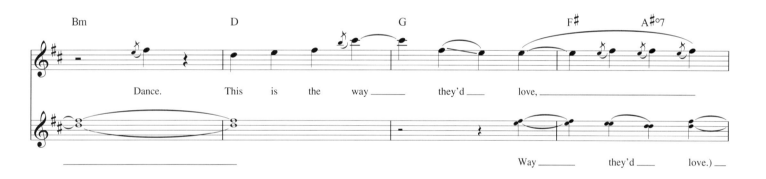

Dance. This is the way _____ they'd _____ love, _____

Way _____ they'd _____ love.) ___

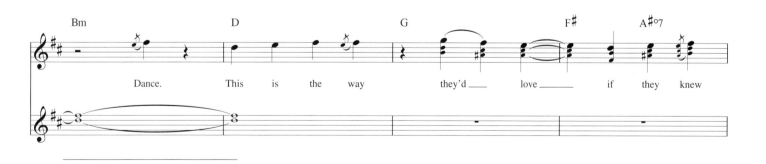

Dance. This is the way they'd _____ love _____ if they knew

Gtrs. 3 & 4: w/ Rhy. Fig. 2

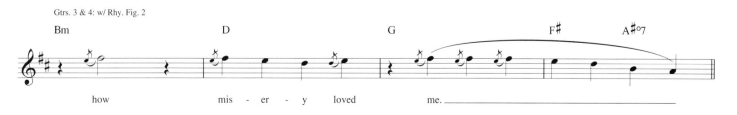

how mis - er - y loved me. _____

**Interlude**

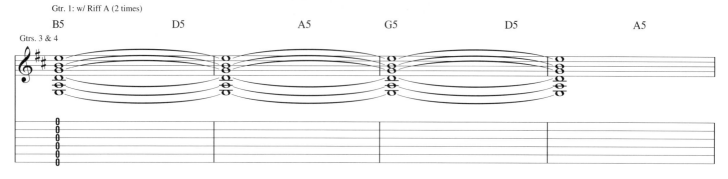

**Outro**

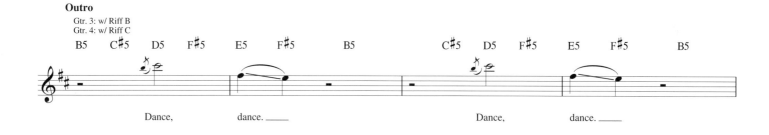

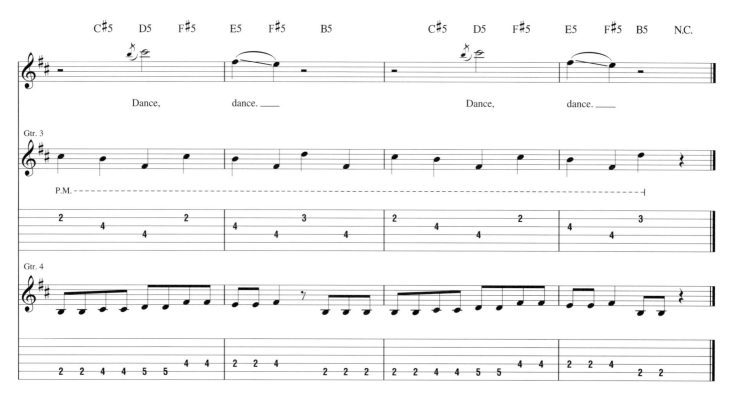

# Sugar, We're Goin' Down

**Words and Music by Patrick Stumph, Peter Wentz, Andrew Hurley and Joseph Trohman**

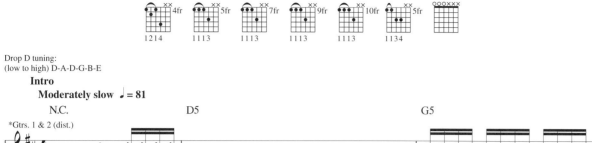

Drop D tuning:
(low to high) D-A-D-G-B-E

**Intro**

**Moderately slow** ♩ = 81

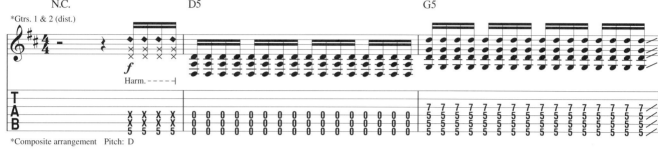

*Composite arrangement   Pitch: D

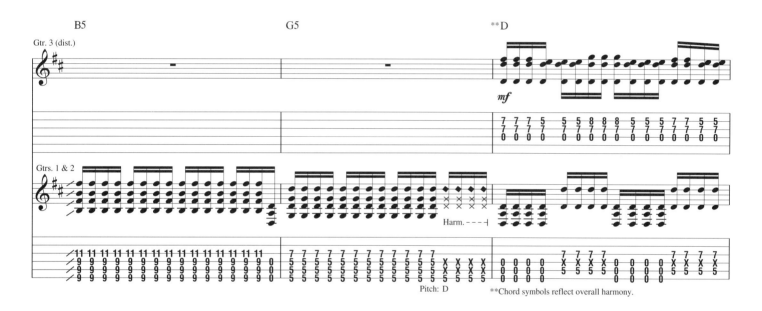

Pitch: D          **Chord symbols reflect overall harmony.

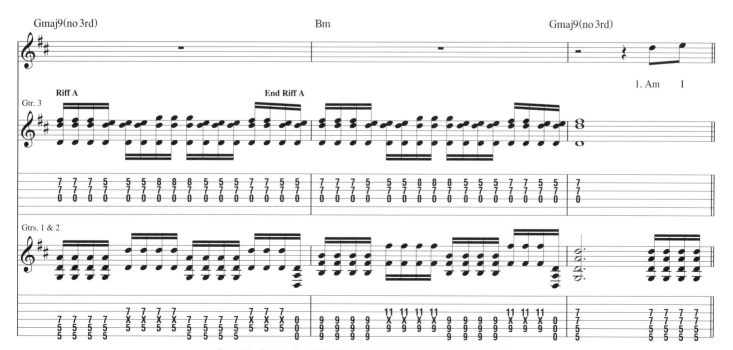

**Verse**

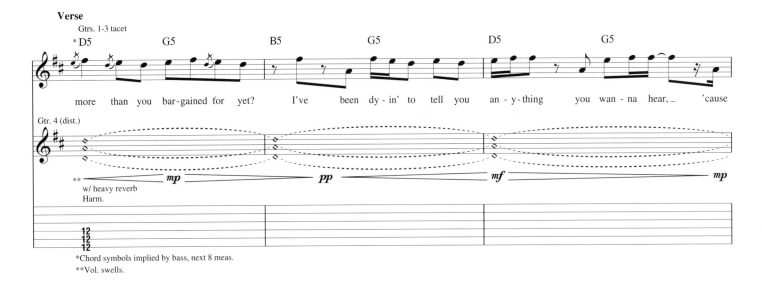

*Chord symbols implied by bass, next 8 meas.
**Vol. swells.

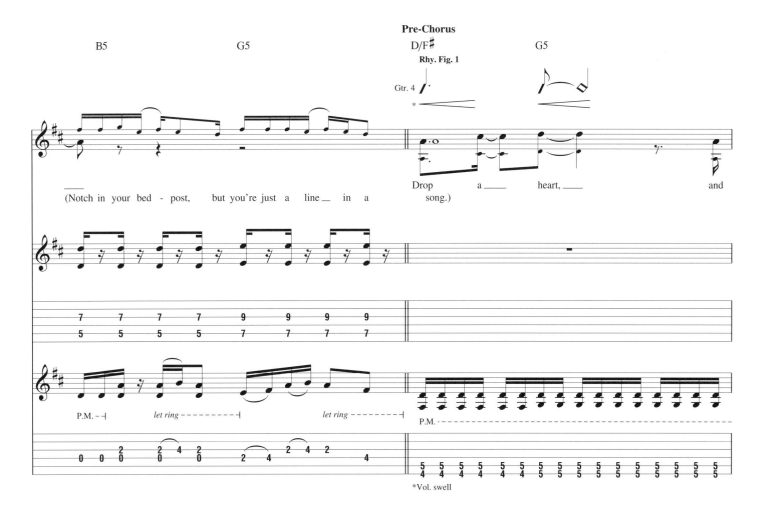

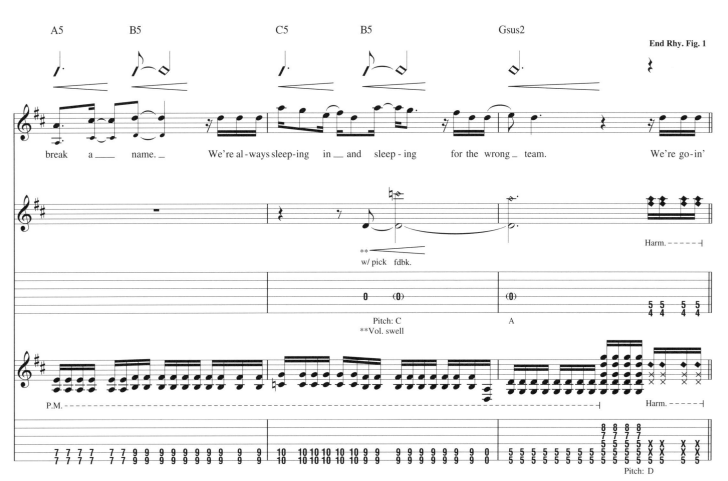

**Chorus**

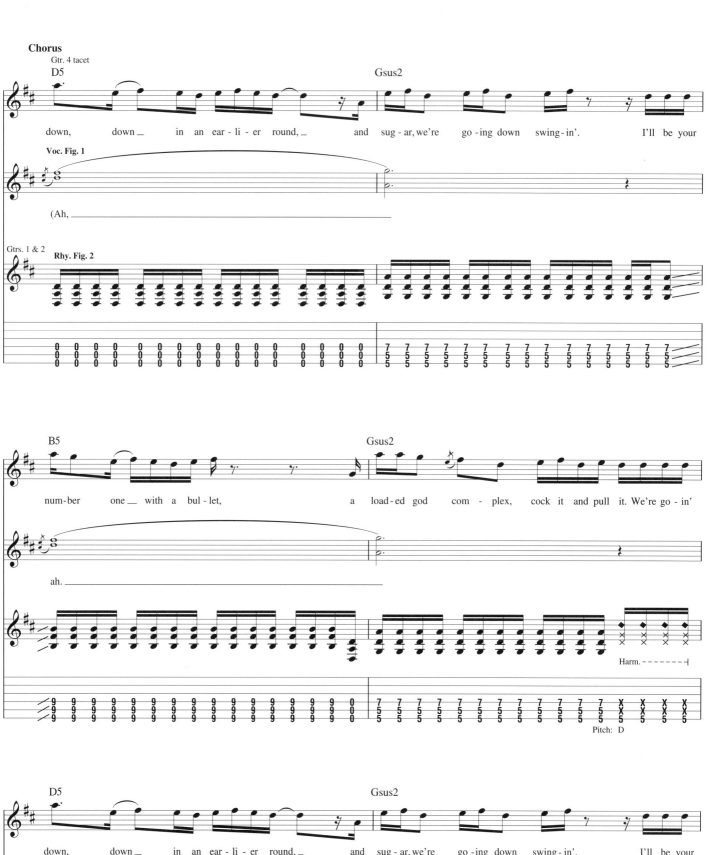

down, down _ in an ear-li-er round, _ and sug-ar, we're go-ing down swing-in'.        I'll be your

(Ah, _

num-ber one _ with a bul-let,        a load-ed god com-plex, cock it and pull it. We're go-in'

ah. _

Pitch: D

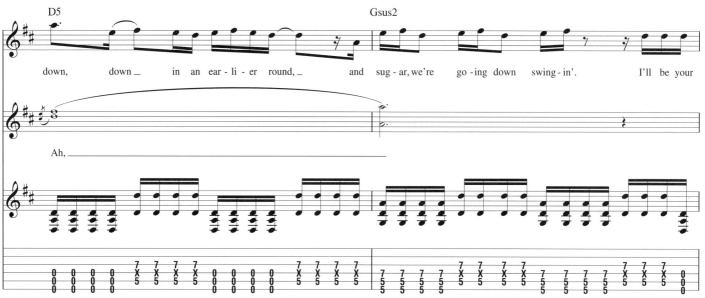

down, down _ in an ear-li-er round, _ and sug-ar, we're go-ing down swing-in'.        I'll be your

Ah, _

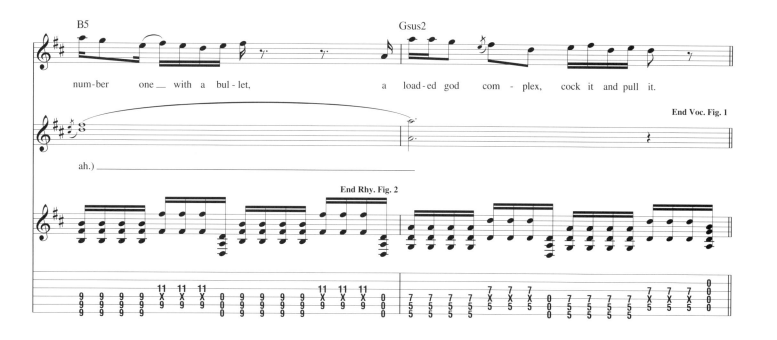

num-ber one __ with a bul - let,      a load-ed god com - plex, cock it and pull it.

**End Voc. Fig. 1**

ah.) _____

**End Rhy. Fig. 2**

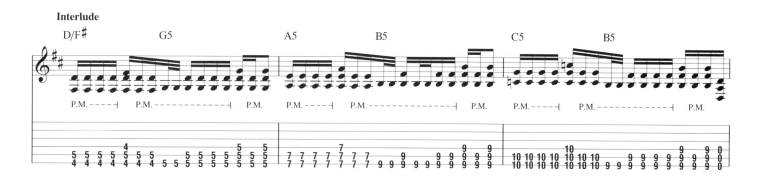

**Interlude**

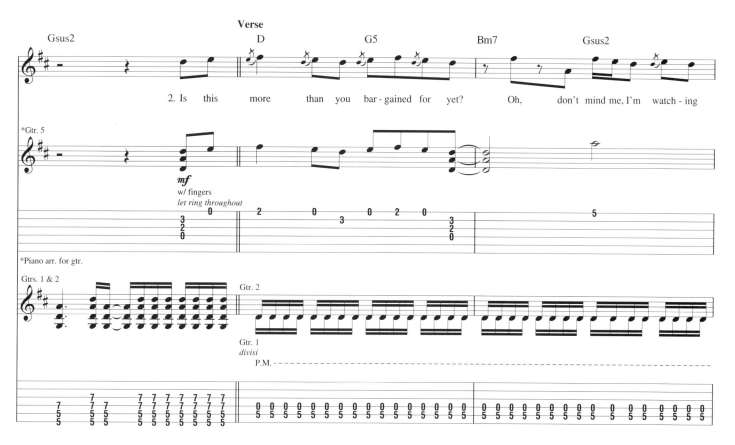

**Verse**

2. Is this more than you bar - gained for yet?      Oh, don't mind me, I'm watch - ing

*Gtr. 5

*mf*
w/ fingers
*let ring throughout*

*Piano arr. for gtr.

Gtrs. 1 & 2

Gtr. 2

Gtr. 1
*divisi*
P.M. - - - - - - - - - - - - - - - - - - - - - - - - - - - - -

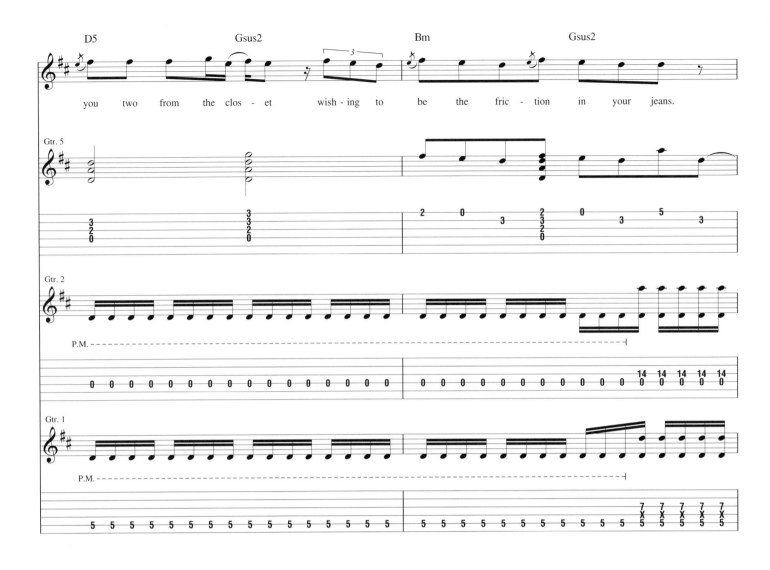

you two from the clos - et wish - ing to be the fric - tion in your jeans.

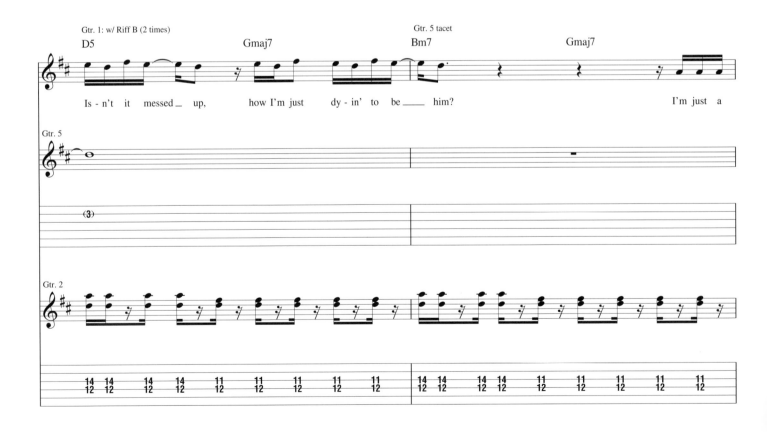

Is - n't it messed __ up, how I'm just dy - in' to be __ him? I'm just a

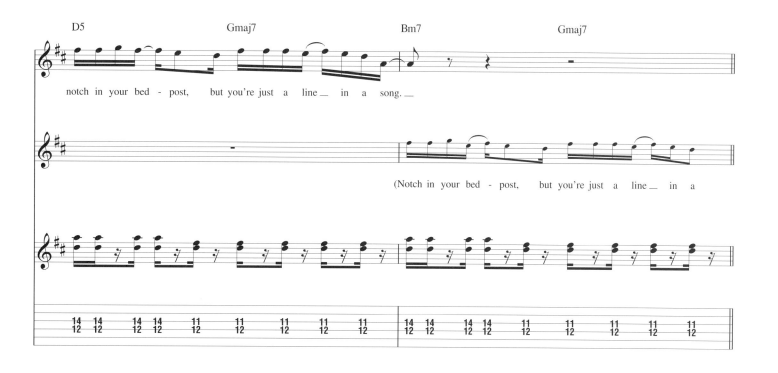

notch in your bed - post, but you're just a line __ in a song. __

(Notch in your bed - post, but you're just a line __ in a

**Pre-Chorus**

Gtr. 4: w/ Rhy. Fig. 1

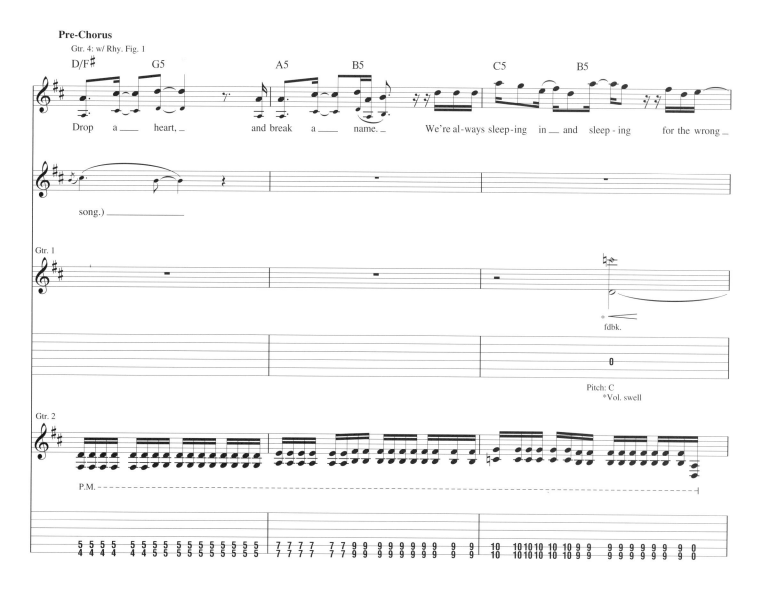

Drop a __ heart, __ and break a __ name. We're al-ways sleep-ing in __ and sleep - ing for the wrong __

song.) __

Gtr. 1

Pitch: C
*Vol. swell

*fdbk.

Gtr. 2

P.M. - - - - - - - - - - - - - - - - - - - - - - - - - - - - - - - - - - - - - - - - - - - - - - - - - - - -|

**Chorus**

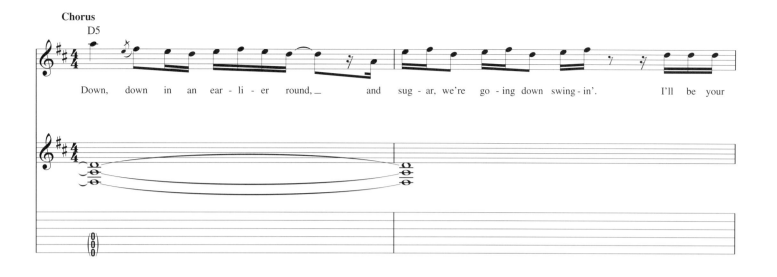

Down, down in an ear-li-er round, _ and sug-ar, we're go-ing down swing-in'. I'll be your

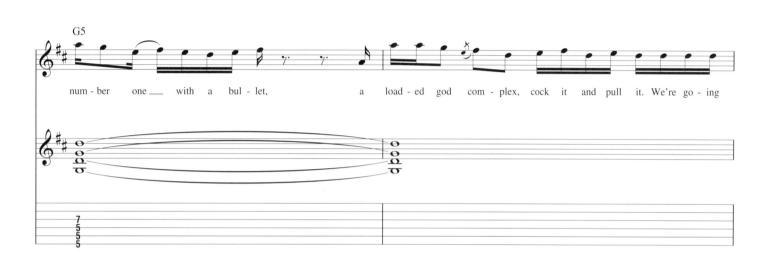

num-ber one _ with a bul-let, a load-ed god com-plex, cock it and pull it. We're go-ing

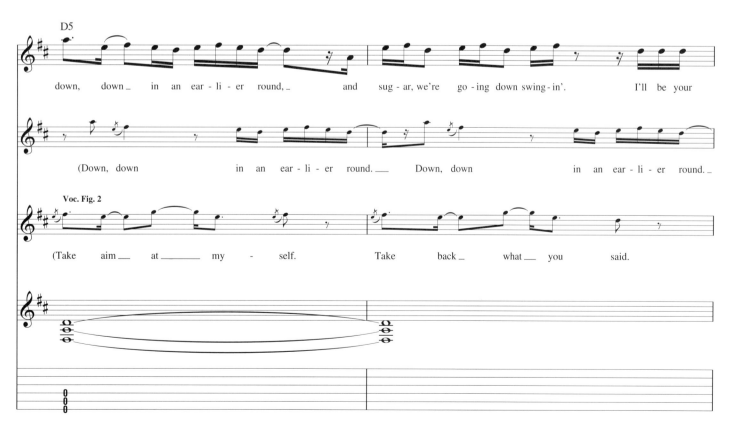

down, down _ in an ear-li-er round, _ and sug-ar, we're go-ing down swing-in'. I'll be your

(Down, down in an ear-li-er round. _ Down, down in an ear-li-er round. _

**Voc. Fig. 2**

(Take aim _ at _ my - self. Take back _ what _ you said.

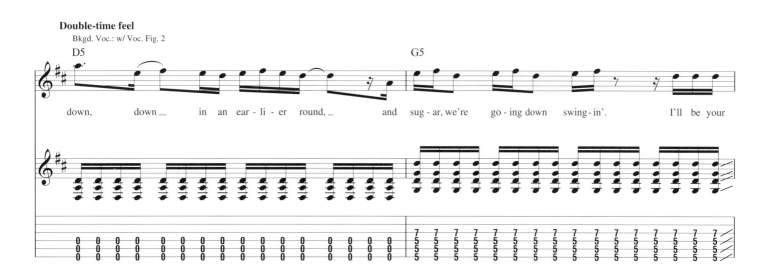

**Double-time feel**
Bkgd. Voc.: w/ Voc. Fig. 2

down, down __ in an ear-li-er round, __ and sug-ar, we're go-ing down swing-in'. I'll be your

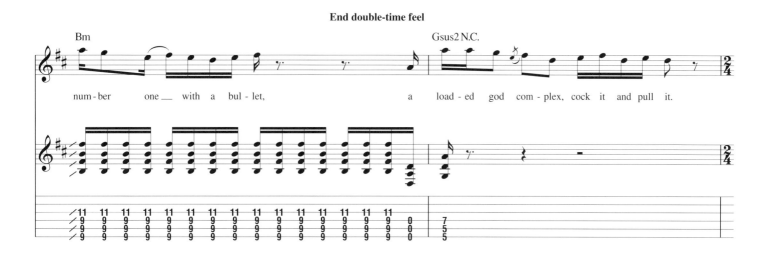

**End double-time feel**

num-ber one __ with a bul-let, a load-ed god com-plex, cock it and pull it.

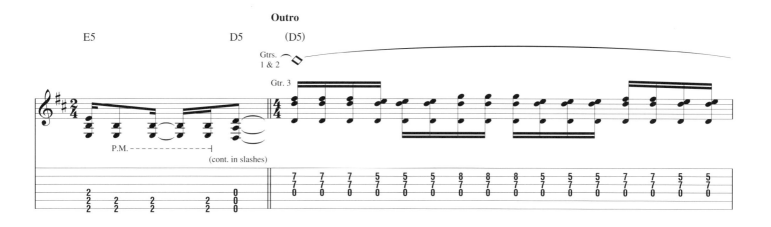

**Outro**

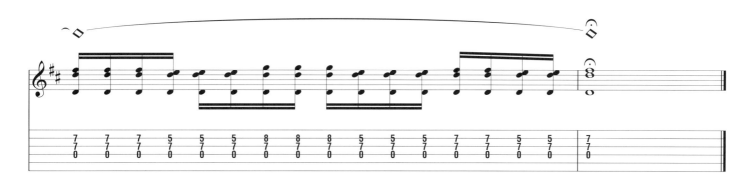

# Nobody Puts Baby in the Corner

**Words and Music by Patrick Stumph, Peter Wentz, Andrew Hurley and Joseph Trohman**

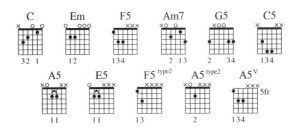

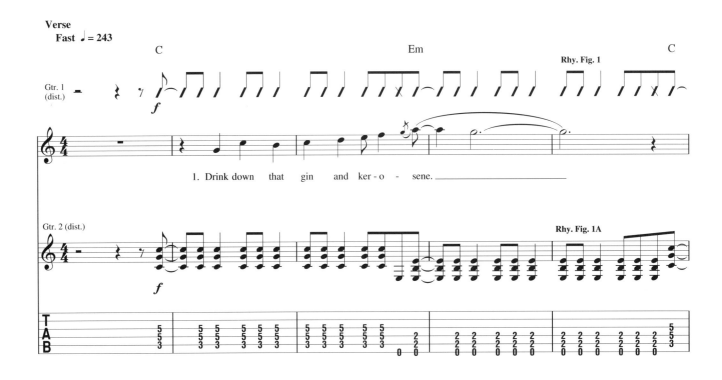

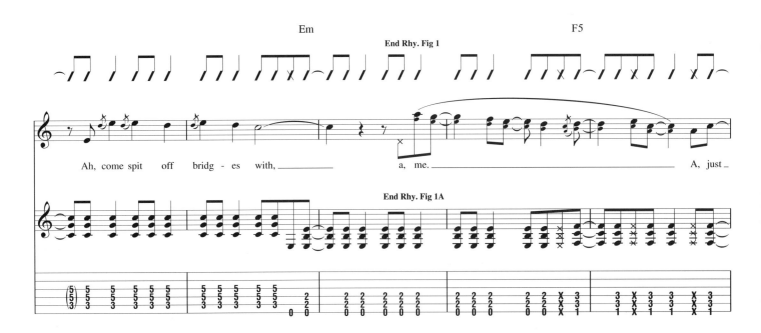

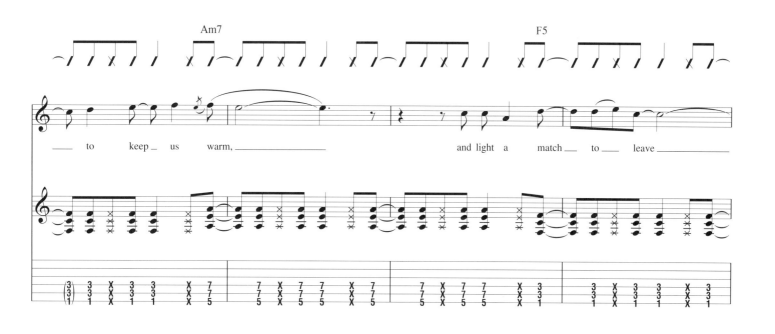

to keep us warm, and light a match to leave

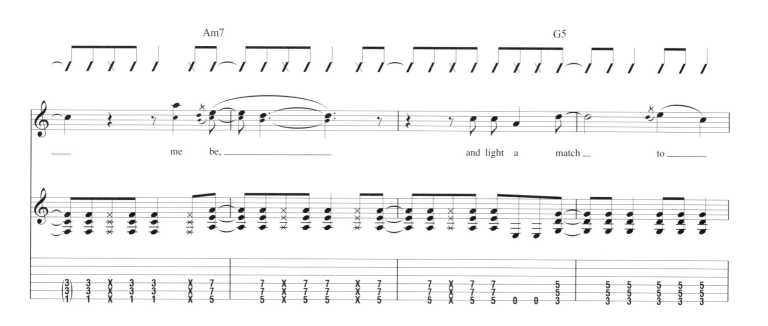

me be, and light a match to

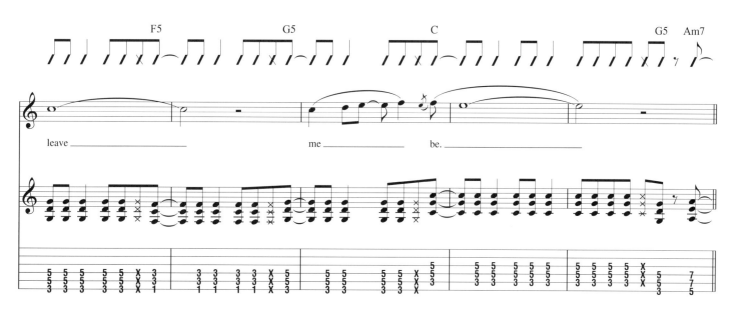

leave me be.

**Verse**

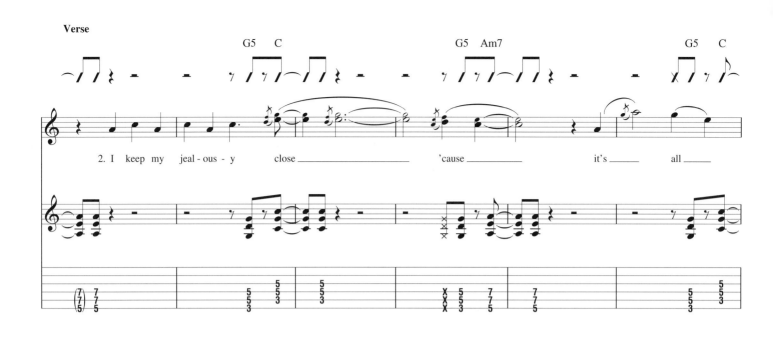

2. I keep my jeal-ous-y close ___ 'cause ___ it's ___ all ___

mine. ___ And if you say this makes you hap-py then I'm not the on-ly

(cont. in notation)

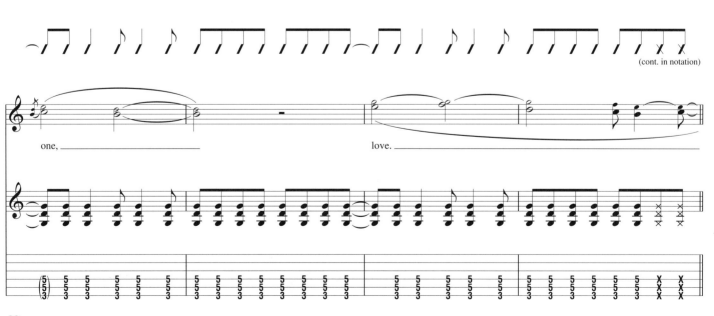

one, ___ love. ___

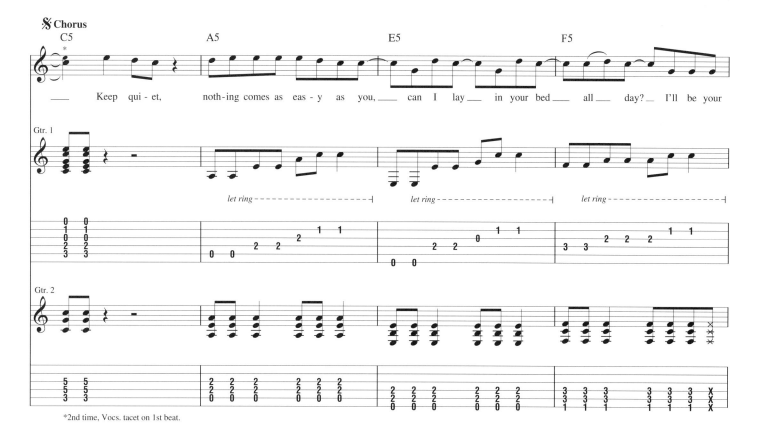

*2nd time, Vocs. tacet on 1st beat.

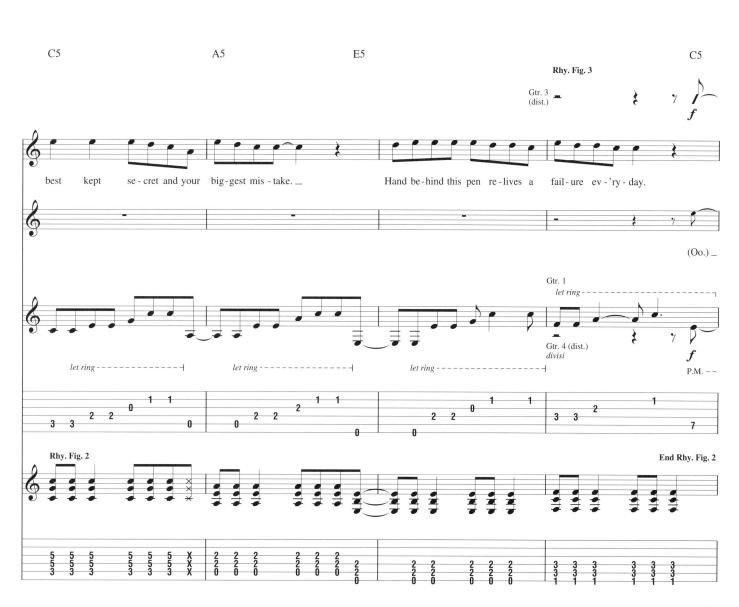

**Half-time feel**

Gtrs. 1 & 2 tacet

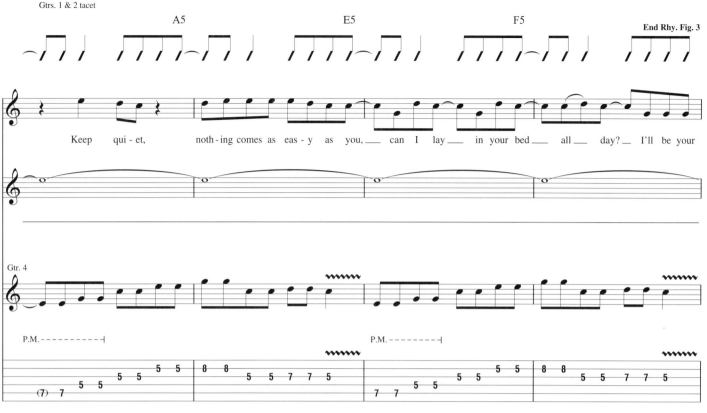

Keep qui - et, noth - ing comes as eas - y as you, __ can I lay __ in your bed __ all __ day? I'll be your

*To Coda* ⊕

**End half-time feel**

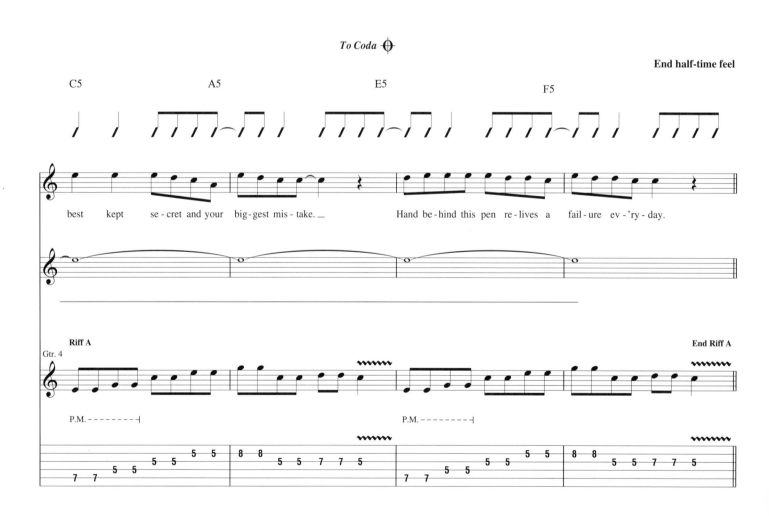

best kept se - cret and your big - gest mis - take. __ Hand be - hind this pen re - lives a fail - ure ev -'ry - day.

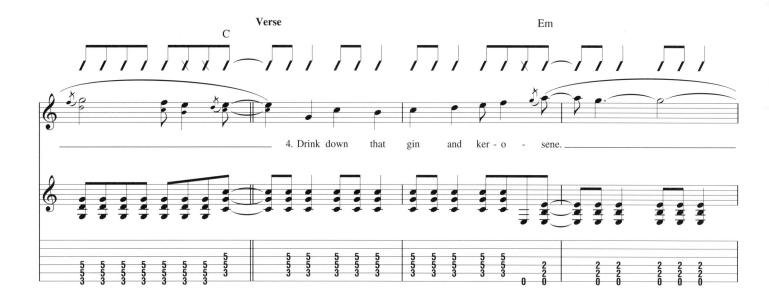

4. Drink down that gin and ker - o - sene.

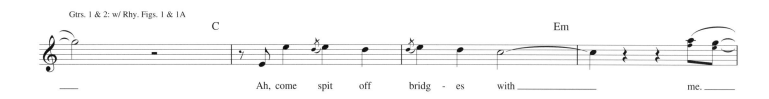

Gtrs. 1 & 2: w/ Rhy. Figs. 1 & 1A

Ah, come spit off bridg - es with _____ me. _____

light a match to leave _____ me be. _____

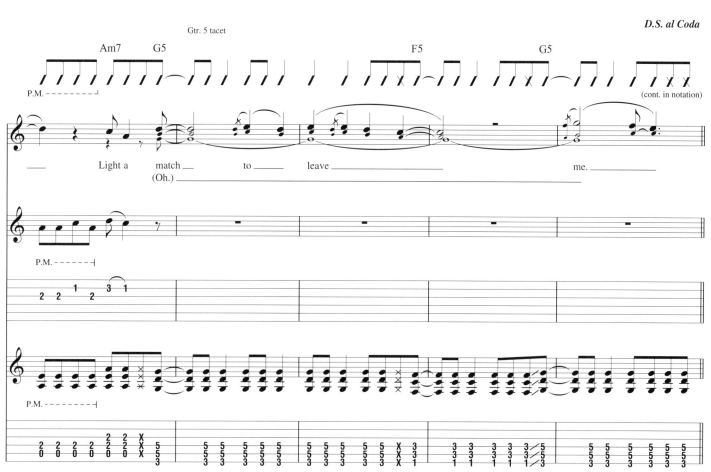

Gtr. 5 tacet

*D.S. al Coda*

Light a match __ to __ leave _____ me. _____
(Oh.) _____

**Coda**

**Interlude**

Gtr. 4 tacet

Gtr. 3 tacet

F5

Am

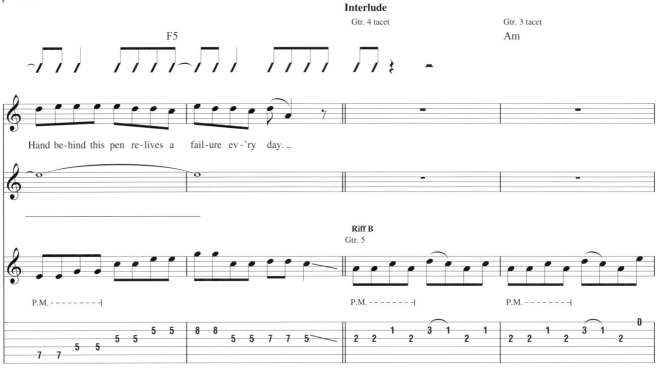

Hand be-hind this pen re-lives a fail-ure ev -'ry day.

**Riff B**
Gtr. 5

P.M.

Gtr. 5: w/ Riff B (2 times)

Gtr. 1

**End Riff B**

Gtr. 2

steady gliss.

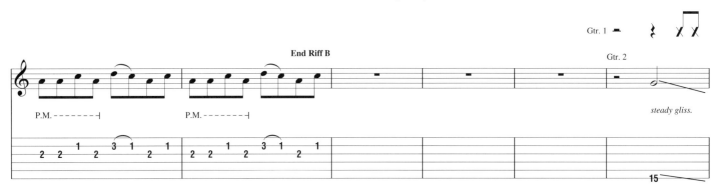

P.M.

P.M.

**Bridge**

Gtr. 5: w/ Riff B (1st 2 meas.)

F5

Am7

F5

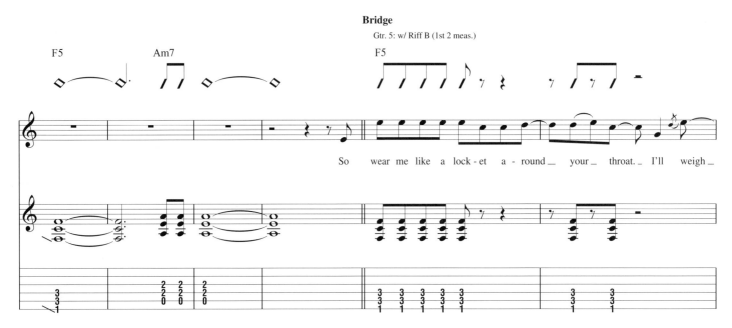

So wear me like a lock-et a -round your throat. I'll weigh

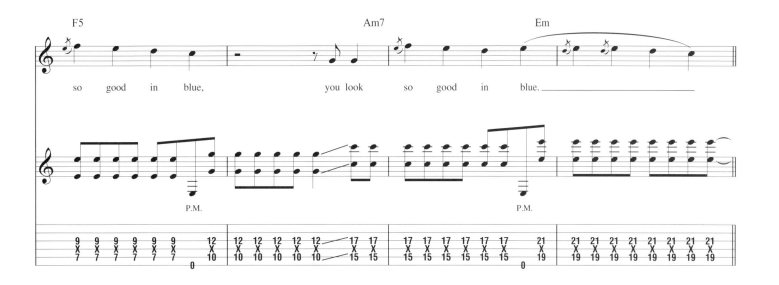

so good in blue, you look so good in blue._____

**Outro-Chorus**

End half-time feel

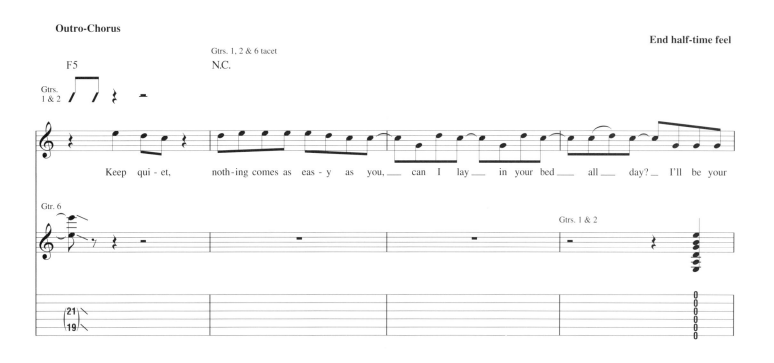

Keep qui - et, noth - ing comes as eas - y as you,__ can I lay __ in your bed __ all __ day? __ I'll be your

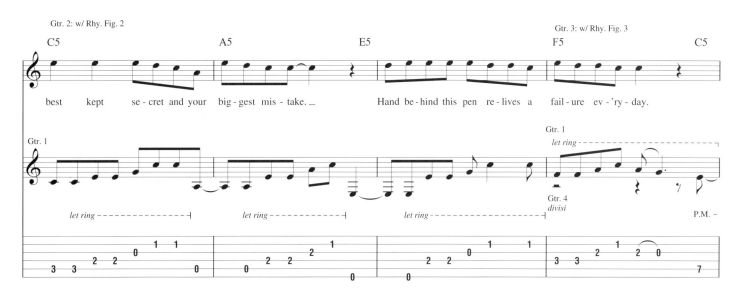

best kept se - cret and your big - gest mis - take. __ Hand be - hind this pen re - lives a fail - ure ev - 'ry - day.

**Half-time feel**

Gtr. 1 tacet

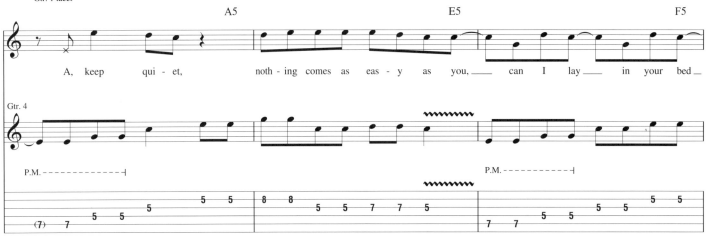

A, keep qui - et, noth - ing comes as eas - y as you, ___ can I lay ___ in your bed ___

Gtr. 4: w/ Riff A (1 1/2 times)

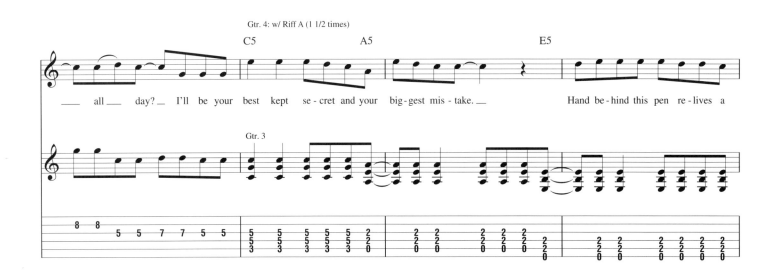

___ all ___ day? ___ I'll be your best kept se - cret and your big - gest mis - take. ___ Hand be - hind this pen re - lives a

**End half-time feel**

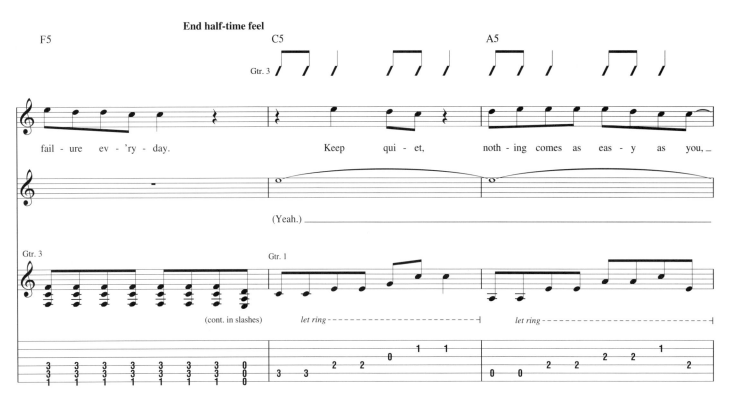

fail - ure ev - 'ry - day. Keep qui - et, noth - ing comes as eas - y as you, ___

(Yeah.) ___

(cont. in slashes)

let ring -------

let ring -------

# I've Got a Dark Alley and a Bad Idea That Says You Should Shut Your Mouth
## (Summer Song)

**Words and Music by Patrick Stumph, Peter Wentz, Andrew Hurley and Joseph Trohman**

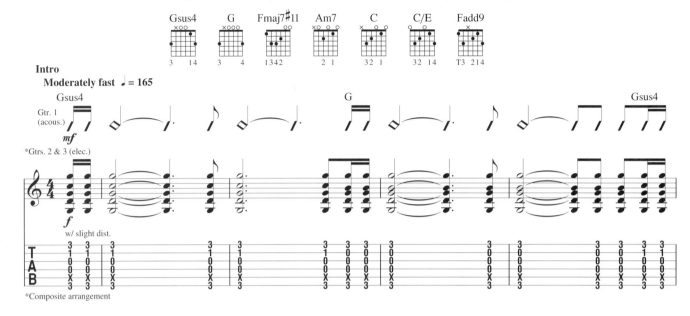

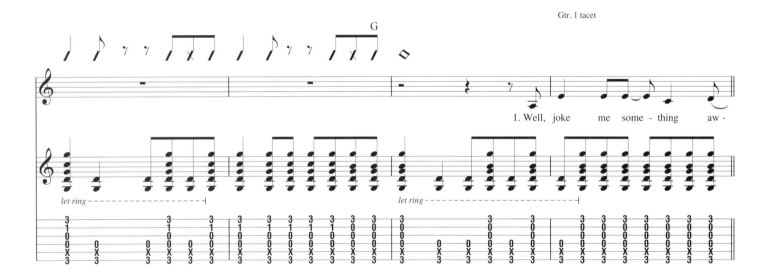

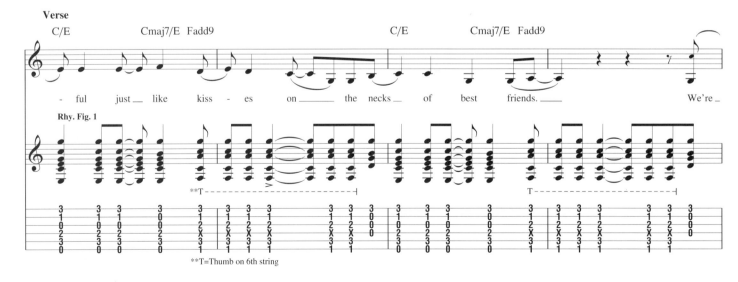

the kids _____ who feel _____ like dead ends. _____ And I

**End Rhy. Fig. 1**

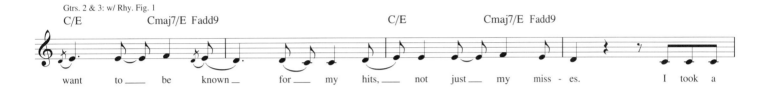

want to _____ be known _____ for my hits, _____ not just _____ my miss - es. I took a

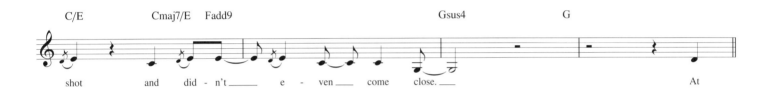

shot and did - n't _____ e - ven _____ come close. _____ At

**Pre-Chorus**

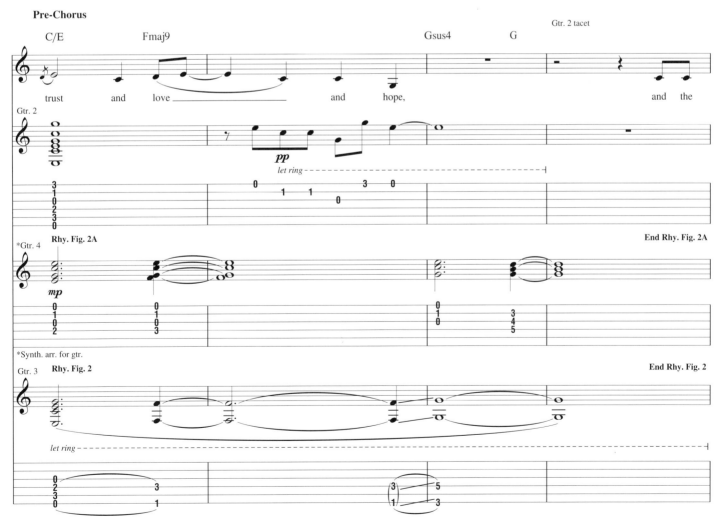

trust and love _____ and hope, and the

55

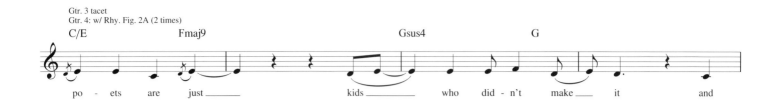

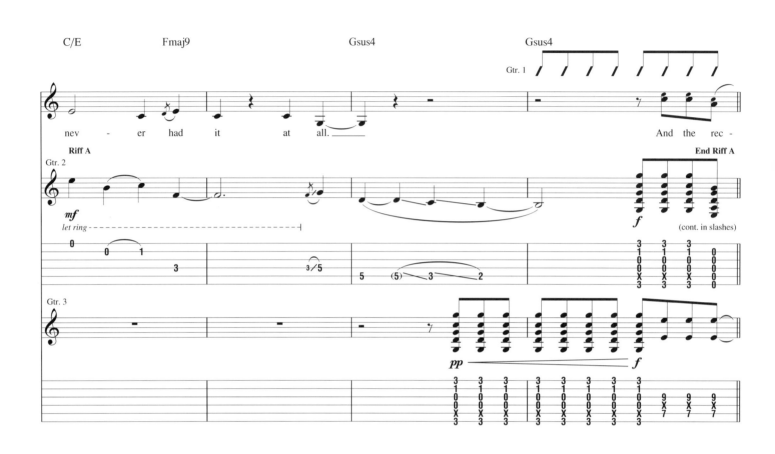

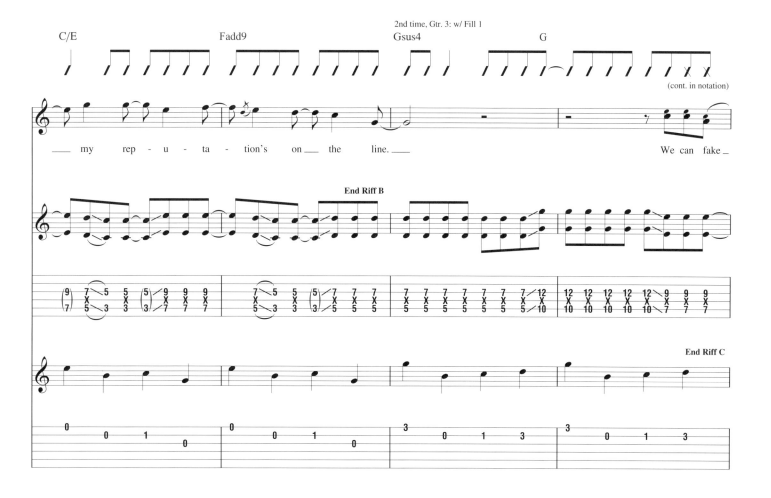

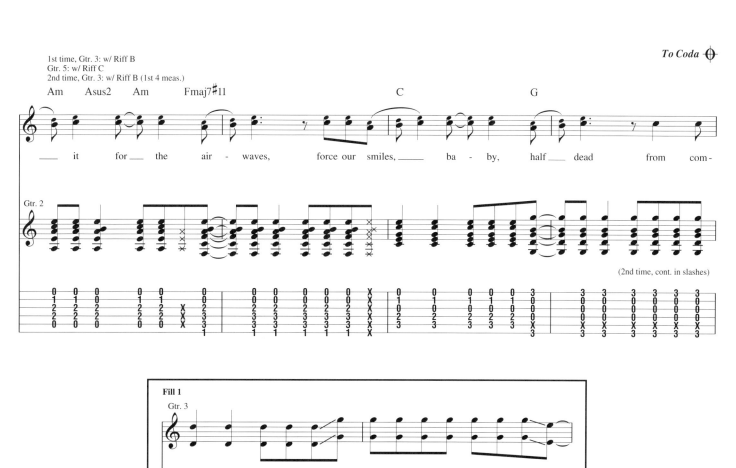

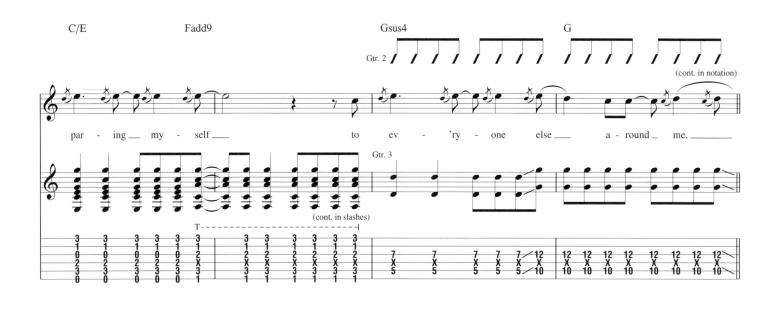

par - ing my - self \_\_ to ev - 'ry - one else \_\_ a - round \_\_ me. \_\_

**Interlude**

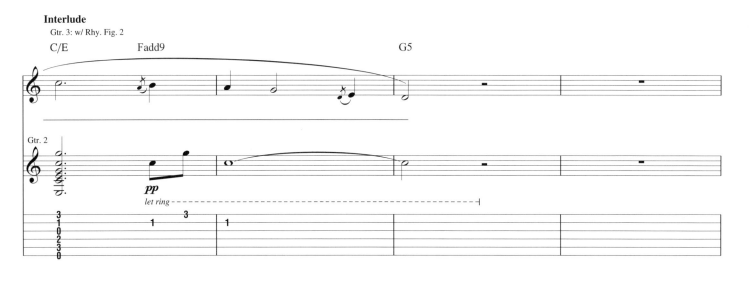

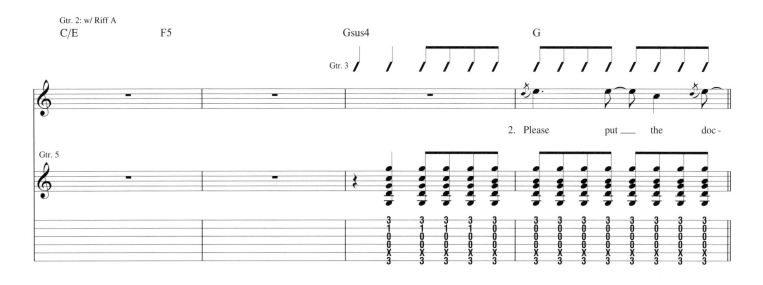

2. Please put \_\_ the doc -

**Verse**

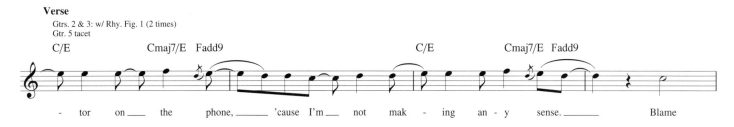

- tor on \_\_ the phone, \_\_ 'cause I'm not mak - ing an - y sense. \_\_ Blame

ev - 'ry - one _____ but me _____ for this mess. _____ And my

back has _____ been break - ing _____ from _____ this heav - y heart, _____ and we

nev - er seemed _____ so _____ far. _____ I'm

**Pre-Chorus**

Gtr. 3: w/ Rhy. Fig. 2
Gtr. 4: w/ Rhy. Fig. 2A (2 times)

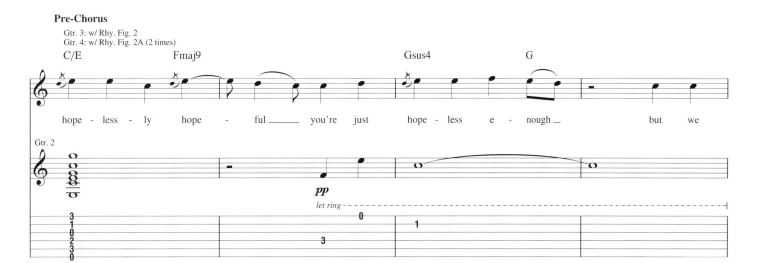

hope - less - ly hope - ful _____ you're just hope - less e - nough _____ but we

*D.S. al Coda*

Gtr. 2: w/ Riff A

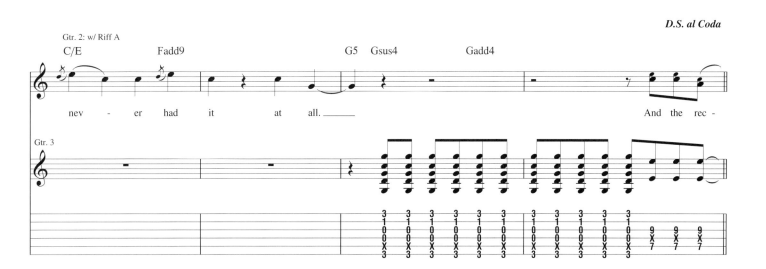

nev - er had it at all. _____ And the rec -

## ⊕ Coda

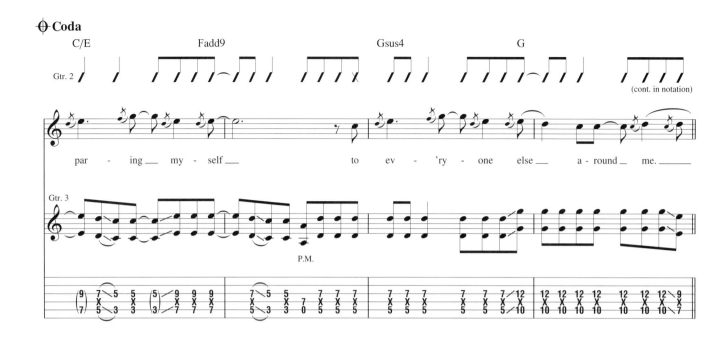

par - ing ___ my - self ___ to ev - 'ry - one else ___ a - round ___ me. ___

## Outro

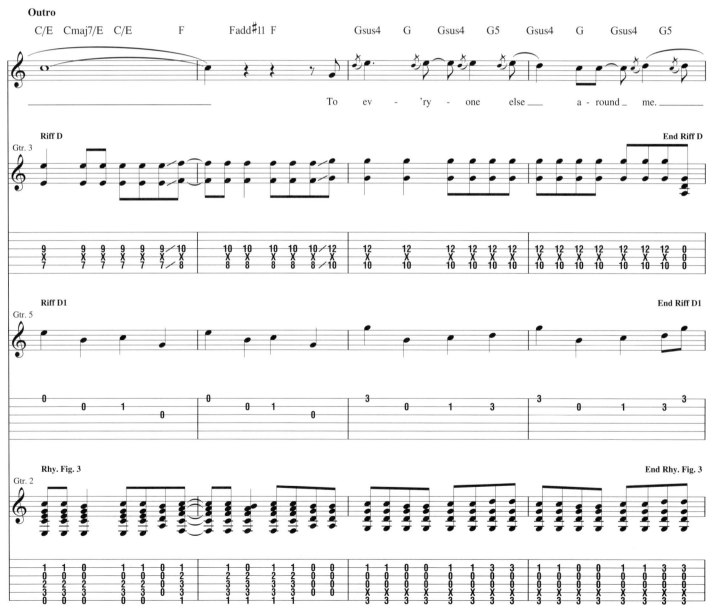

To ev - 'ry - one else ___ a - round ___ me. ___

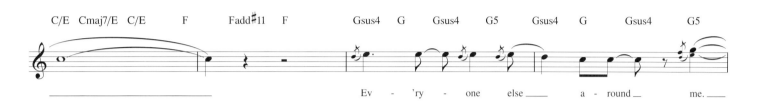

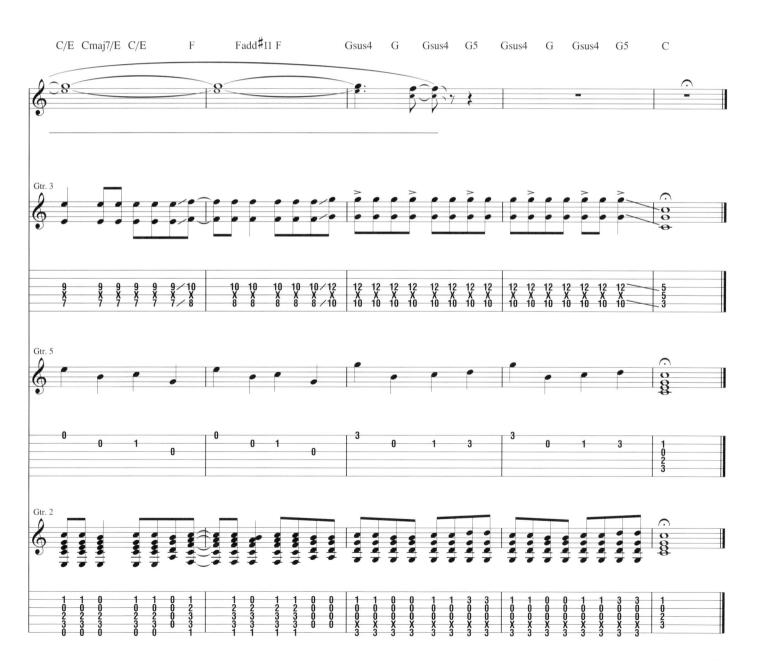

# 7 Minutes in Heaven

## (Atavan Halen)

**Words and Music by Patrick Stumph, Peter Wentz, Andrew Hurley and Joseph Trohman**

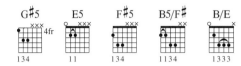

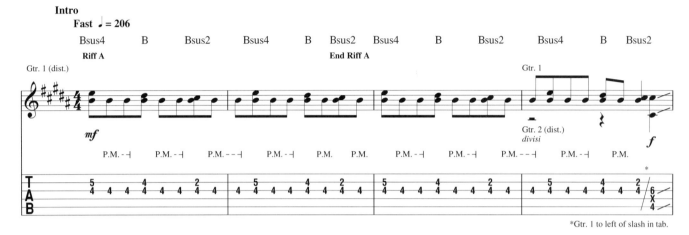

*Gtr. 1 to left of slash in tab.

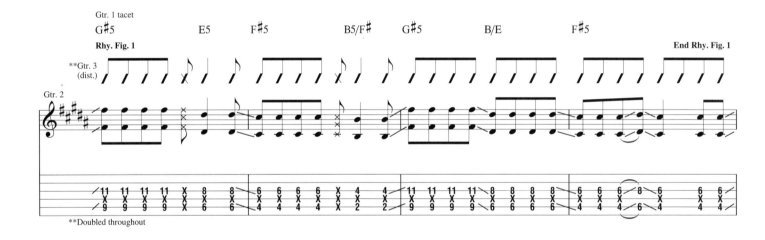

**Doubled throughout

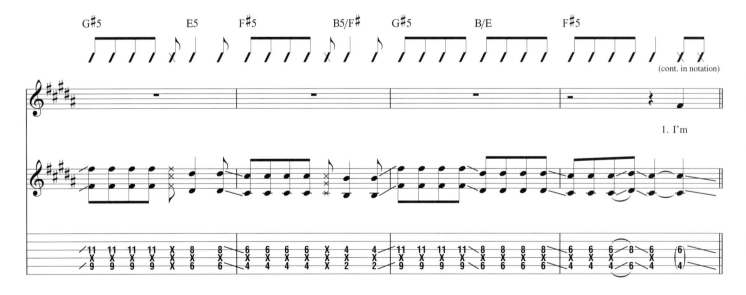

**Verse**

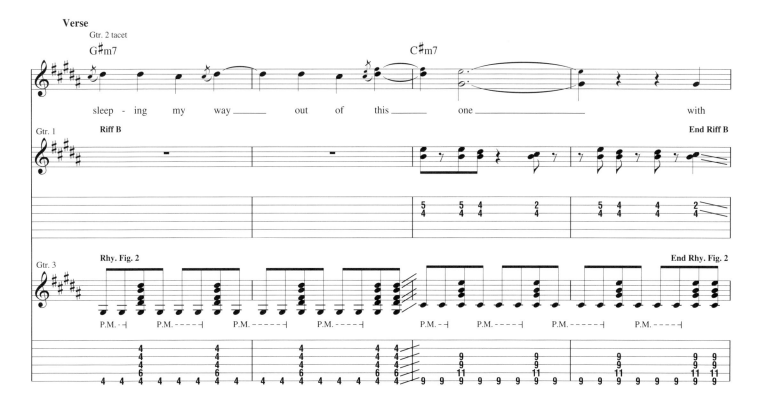

sleep - ing my way out of this one with

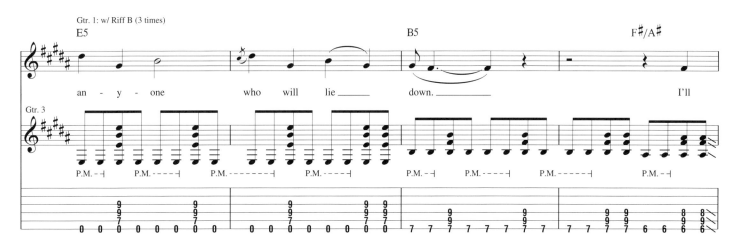

an - y - one who will lie down. I'll

be stuck fix - at - ed on one star when the

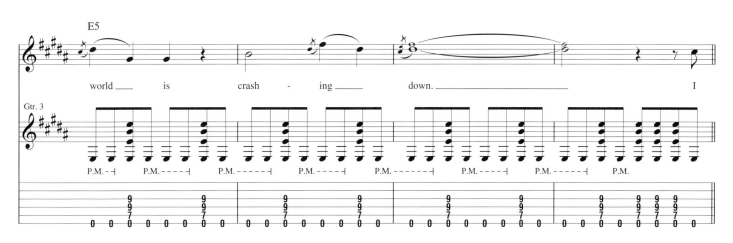

world is crash - ing down. I

keep tell-ing my-self, __ I keep tell-ing my-self I'm not the des-p'rate type.

(But you've got me look-ing in through

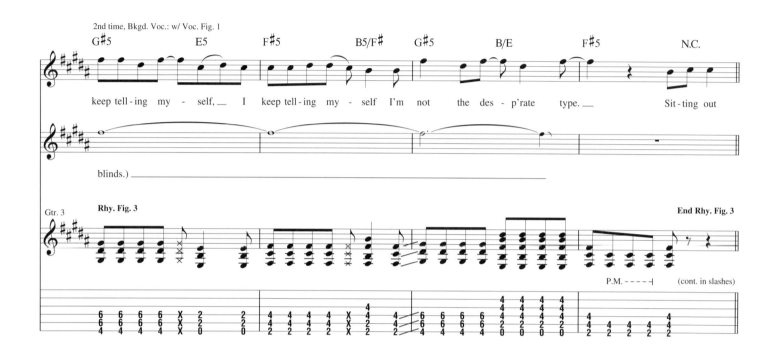

keep tell-ing my-self, __ I keep tell-ing my-self I'm not the des-p'rate type. __ Sit-ting out

blinds.) _____

**Chorus**

**Half-time feel**

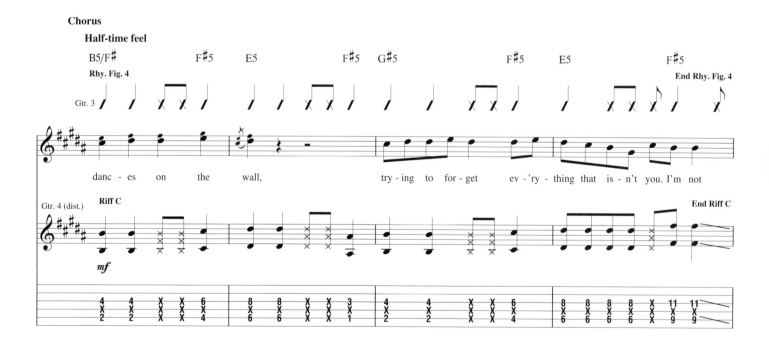

danc-es on the wall, try-ing to for-get ev'-ry-thing that is-n't you. I'm not

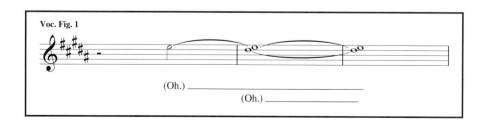

(Oh.) _____
(Oh.) _____

1st time, Gtr. 3: w/ Rhy. Fig. 4 (3 times)
Gtr. 4: w/ Riff C (2 times)
2nd time, Gtr. 3: w/ Rhy. Fig. 4 (2 1/2 times)

go - ing home a - lone        'cause I don't do too well.  I'm sit - ting out

danc - es on the wall,        try - ing to for - get ev - 'ry - thing that is - n't you. I'm not

*To Coda* ⊕

End half-time feel

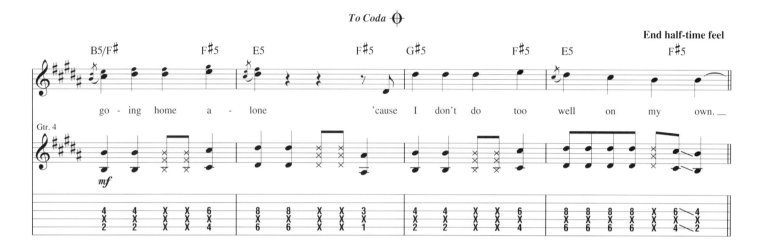

go - ing home a - lone        'cause I don't do too well on my own. __

Gtr. 4

*mf*

**Interlude**

Gtr. 3: w/ Rhy. Fig. 1 (2 times)
Gtr. 4 tacet

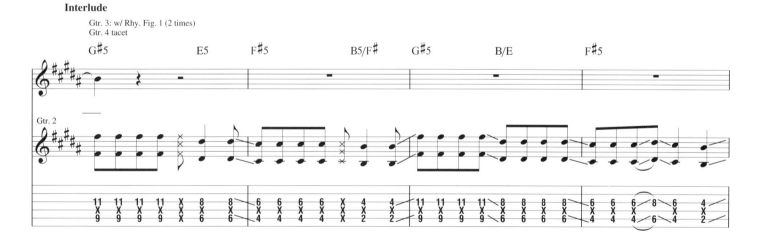

Gtr. 2

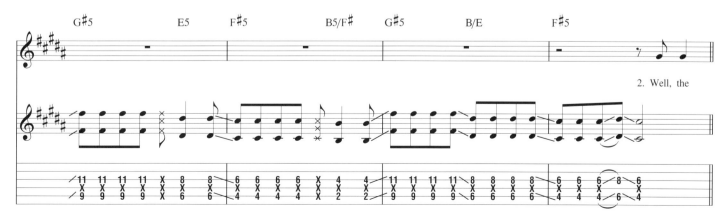

2. Well, the

**Verse**

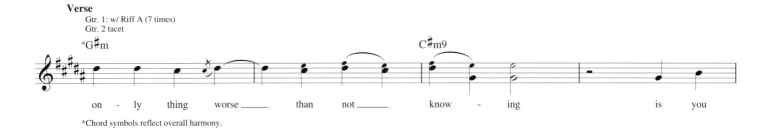

Gtr. 1: w/ Riff A (7 times)
Gtr. 2 tacet

*G#m    C#m9

on - ly thing worse ___ than not ___ know - ing is you

*Chord symbols reflect overall harmony.

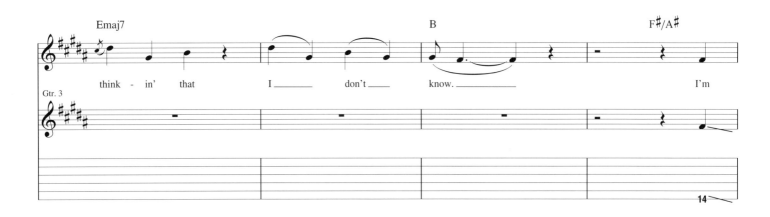

Emaj7    B    F#/A#

think - in' that I ___ don't ___ know. ___ I'm

Gtr. 3

14

Gtr. 3: w/ Rhy. Fig. 2

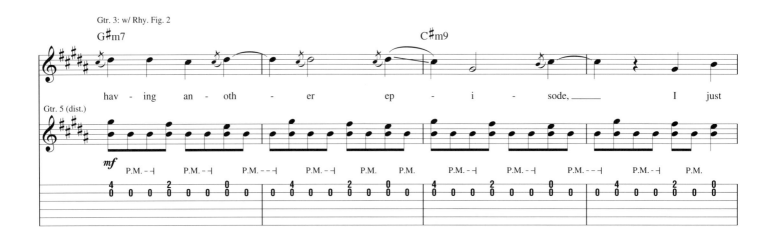

G#m7    C#m9

hav - ing an - oth - er ep - i - sode, ___ I just

Gtr. 5 (dist.)

*mf*  P.M. P.M. P.M. P.M. P.M. P.M. P.M. P.M. P.M. P.M. P.M.

***D.S. al Coda***

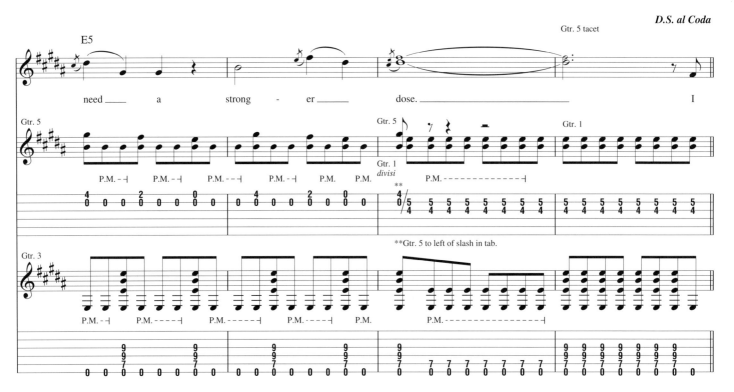

Gtr. 5 tacet

E5

need ___ a strong - er ___ dose. ___ I

Gtr. 5

Gtr. 5    Gtr. 1

P.M. P.M. P.M. P.M. P.M. P.M.    Gtr. 1 *divisi*    P.M.

**  **Gtr. 5 to left of slash in tab.

Gtr. 3

P.M. P.M. P.M. P.M. P.M. P.M.

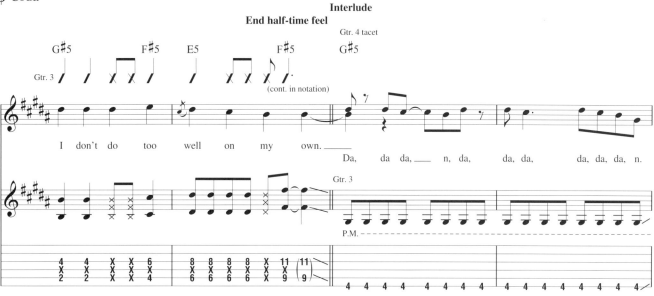

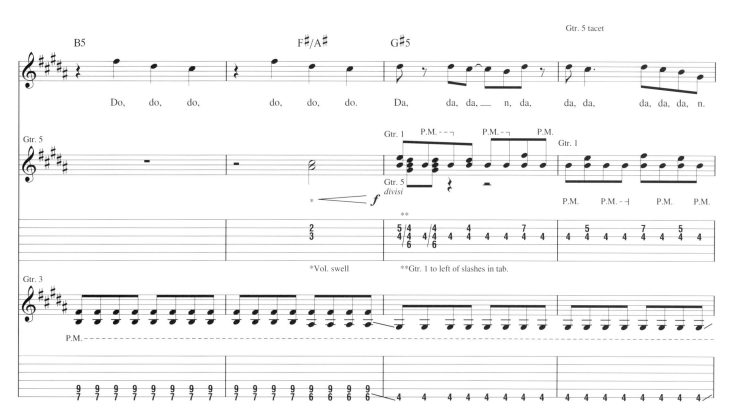

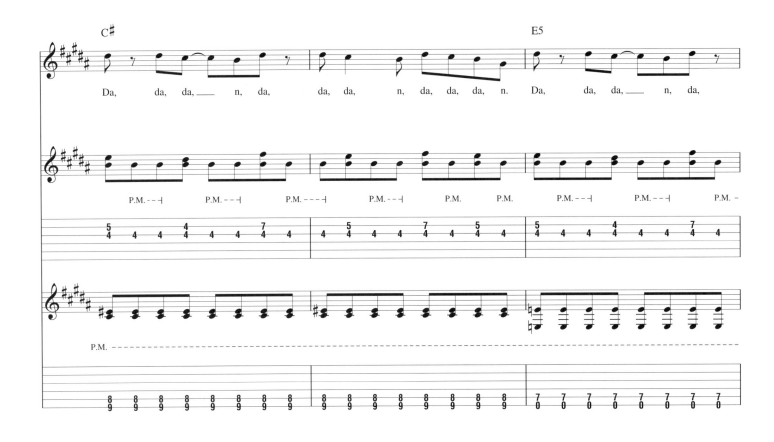

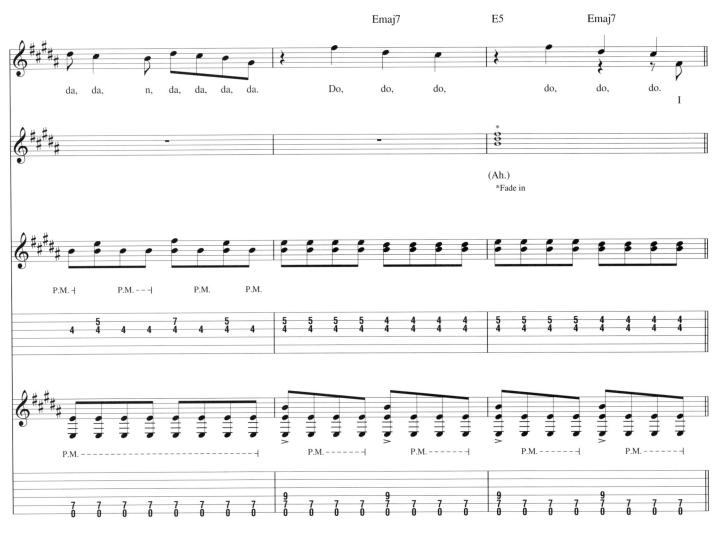

**Pre-Chorus**

keep tell - ing my - self, \_\_ I keep tell - ing my - self I'm not the des - p'rate type.

**Half-time feel**

Bkgd. Voc.: w/ Voc. Fig. 1
Gtr. 3: w/ Rhy. Fig. 1 (2 times)

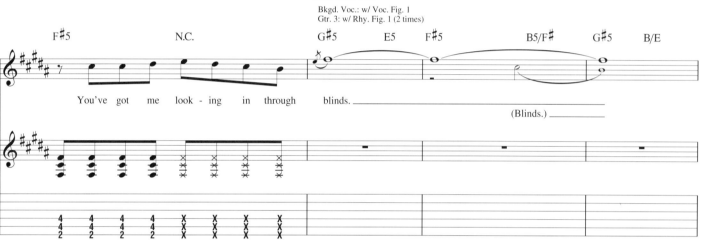

You've got me look - ing in through blinds. _____

(Blinds.) \_\_\_\_\_

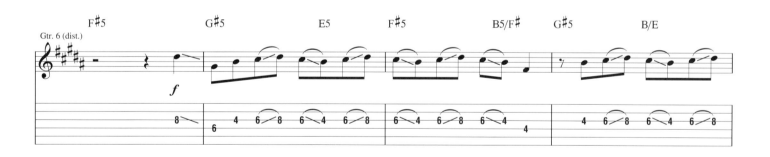

Gtr. 3: w/ Rhy. Fig. 3

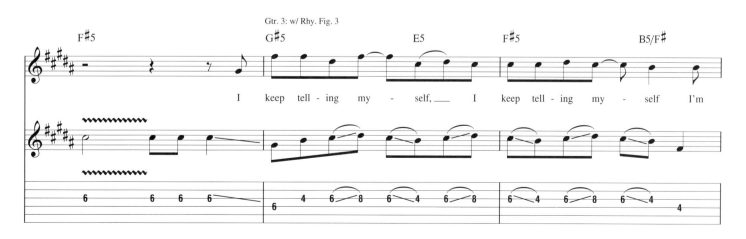

I keep tell - ing my - self, \_\_ I keep tell - ing my - self I'm

**Outro-Chorus**

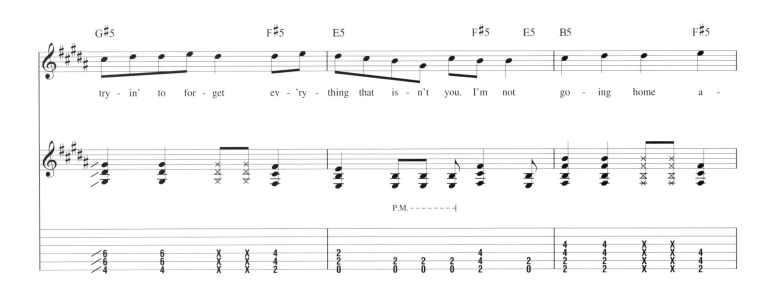

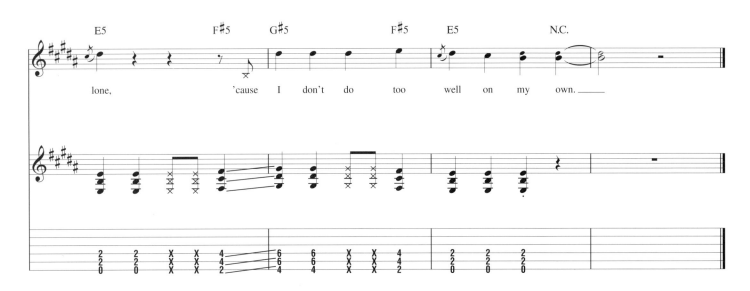

# Sophomore Slump or Comeback of the Year

Words and Music by Patrick Stumph, Peter Wentz, Andrew Hurley and Joseph Trohman

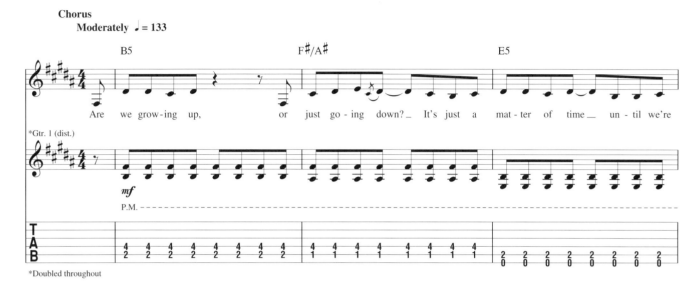

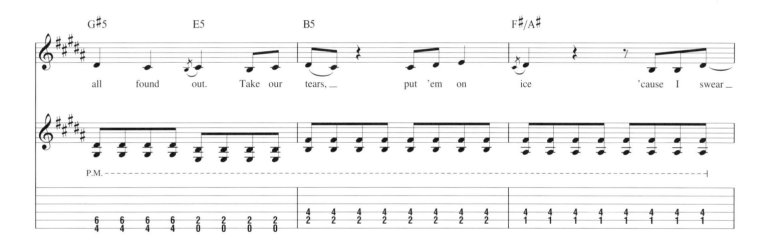

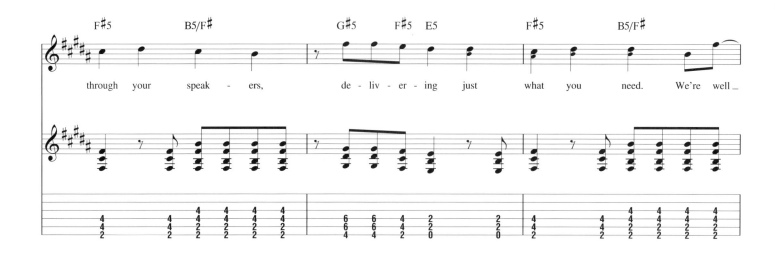

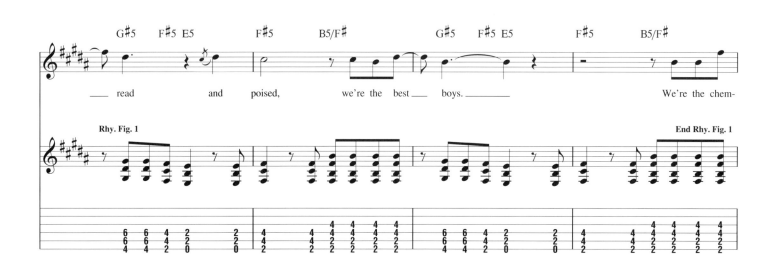

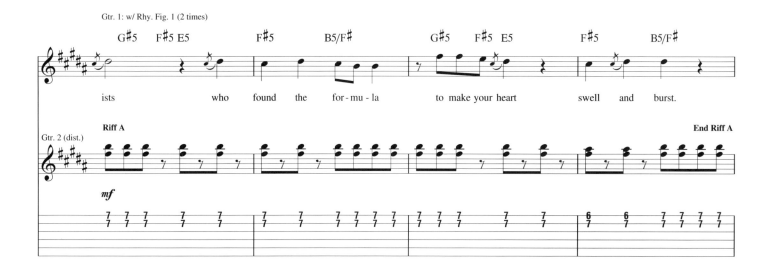

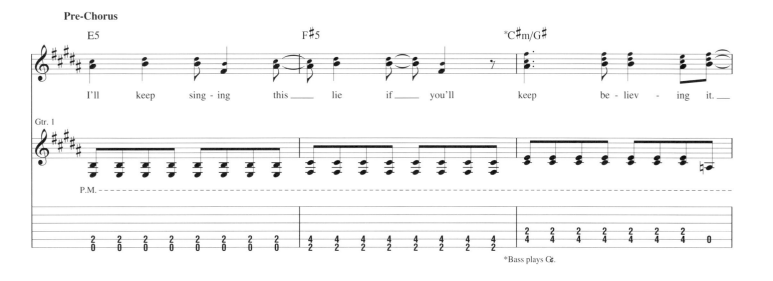

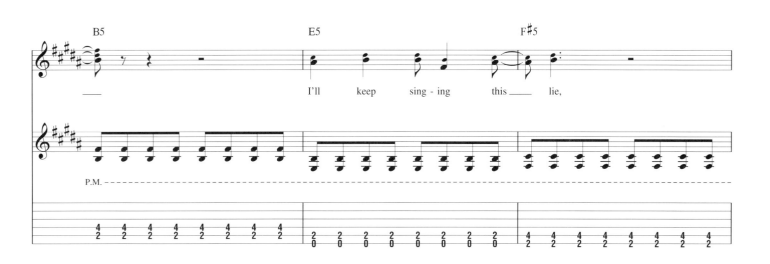

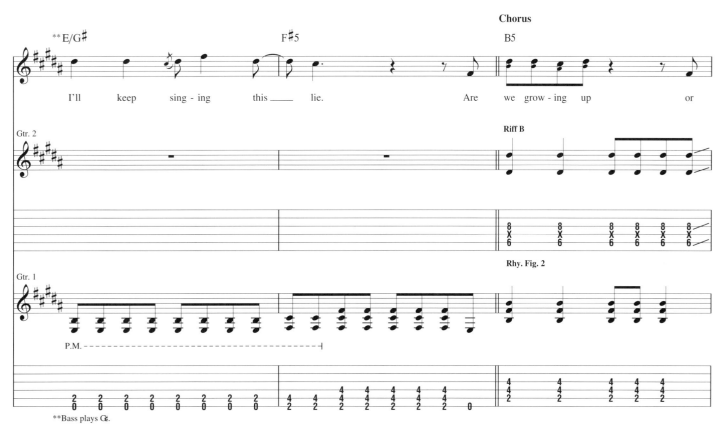

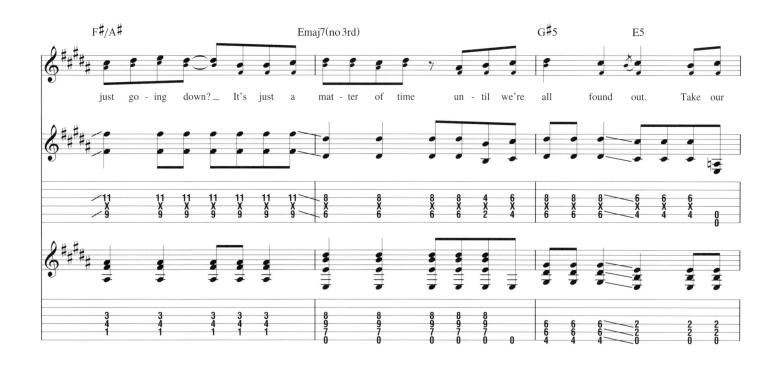

just go-ing down?_ It's just a mat-ter of time un-til we're all found out. Take our

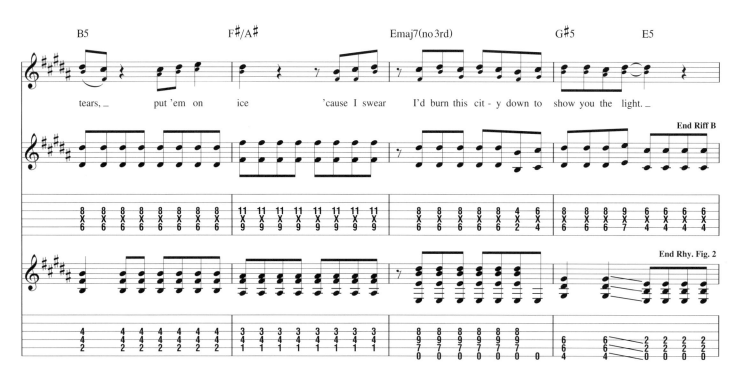

tears,_ put 'em on ice 'cause I swear I'd burn this cit-y down to show you the light._

End Riff B

End Rhy. Fig. 2

**Verse**

Gtr. 2 tacet

Gtr. 1 tacet

2. And we're trav-eled like gyp-sies, on-ly

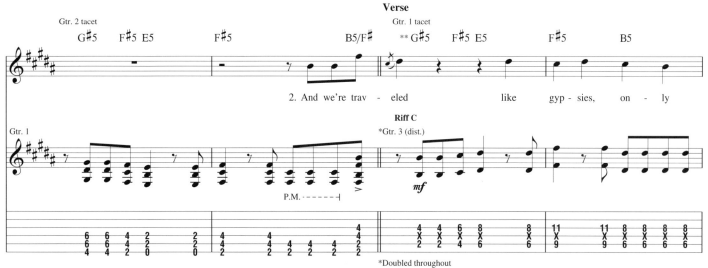

Gtr. 1

**Riff C**

*Gtr. 3 (dist.)

P.M.------‐

*mf*

*Doubled throughout
**Chord symbols implied by bass, next 8 meas.

with worse __ luck and far less gold. We're the kids you used to

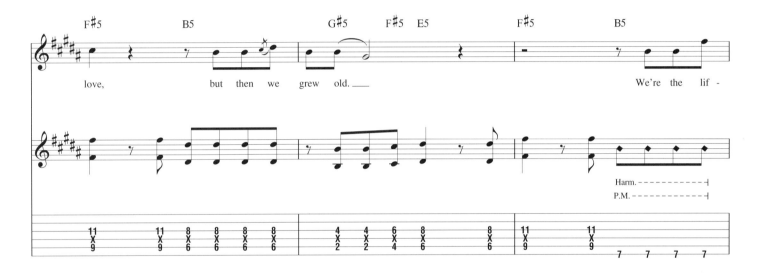

love, but then we grew old. __ We're the lif -

Gtr. 1: w/ Rhy. Fig. 1 (2 times)
Gtr. 2: w/ Riff A (2 times)
Gtr. 3: w/ Riff C (2 times)

ers here 'til the bit - ter end, con - demned from the start.

A - shamed __ of the way the songs and the words own the beat-ing of our __ hearts. 'Cause

**Pre-Chorus**

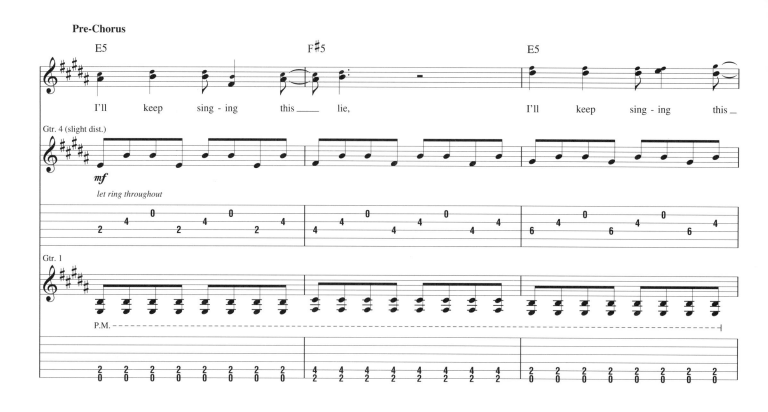

**Chorus**

Gtr. 1: w/ Rhy. Fig. 2
Gtr. 2: w/ Riff B
Gtr. 4 tacet

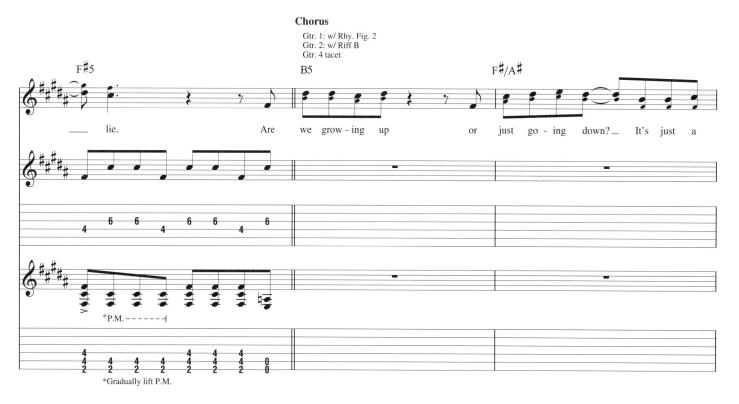

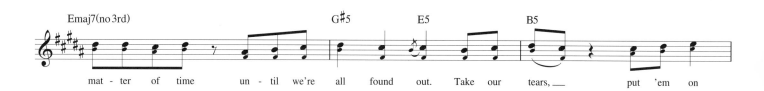

Bridge
Gtr. 2 tacet
B5
F♯/A♯
E5
G♯5
E5
drug in the ther-mo-stat to warm the room up, and there's an - oth - er a - round to help us bend your trust. Got a
Gtr. 4
Riff D
End Riff D
Gtr. 2
Gtr. 1
Rhy. Fig. 3
End Rhy. Fig. 3
Gtr. 1: w/ Rhy. Fig. 3
Gtr. 4: w/ Riff D
B5
F♯/A♯
E5
sun - set in my veins and I need to take a pill to make this
G♯5
E5
B5
town feel o - kay The best part of be -
Gtr. 1
mf
P.M.

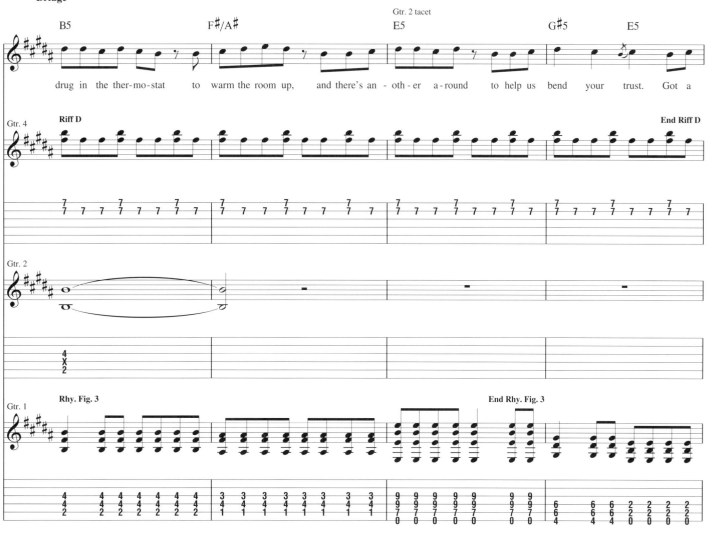

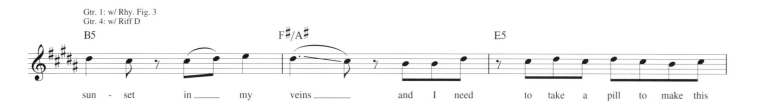

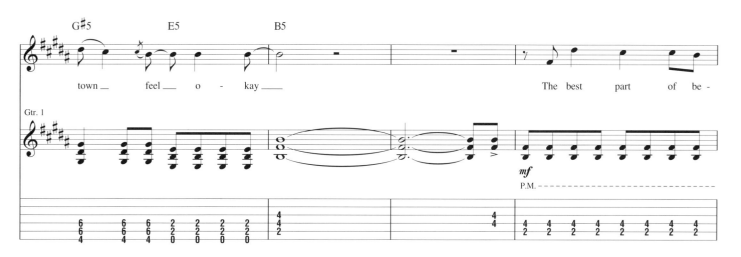

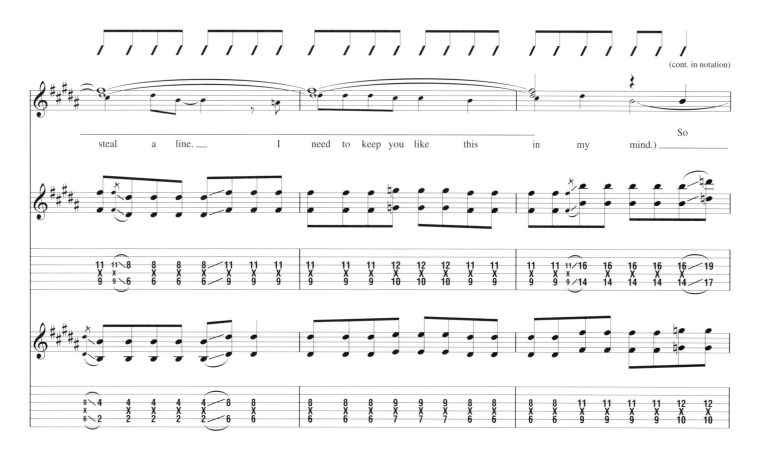

steal a line. ___ I need to keep you like this in my mind.) _____ So

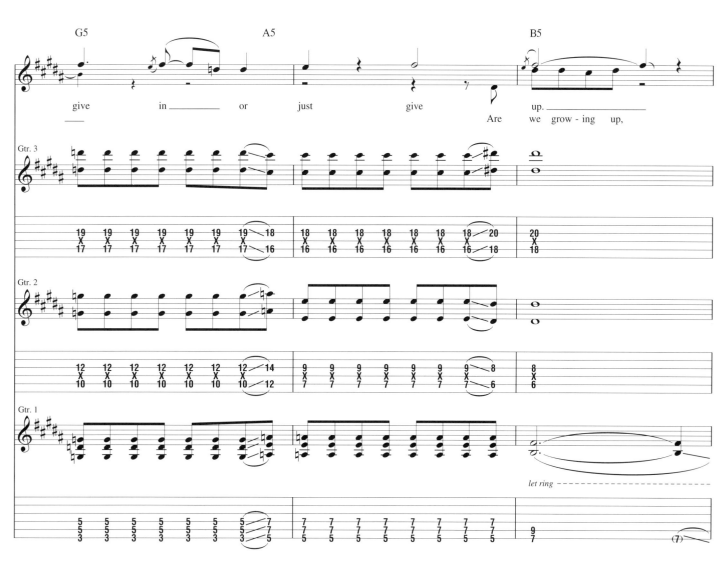

give in _____ or just give up. Are we grow-ing up,

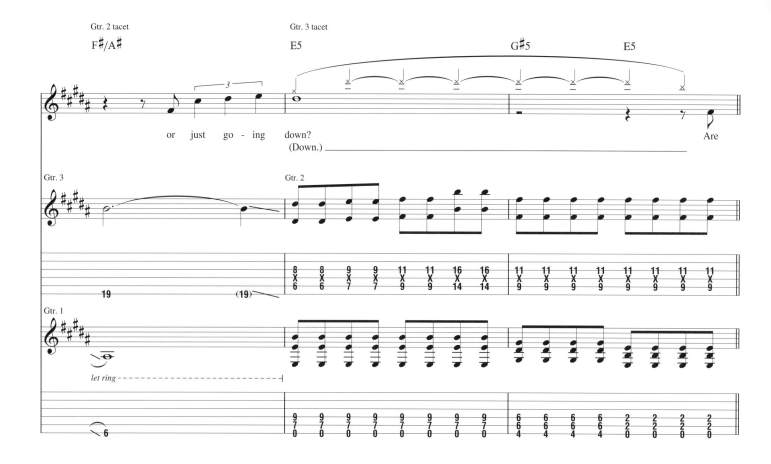

or just go-ing down?
(Down.)

Are

**Outro-Chorus**

Gtr. 1: w/ Rhy. Fig. 2 (1st 6 meas.)
Gtr. 2: w/ Riff B (1st 6 meas.)

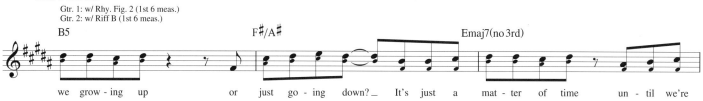

we grow-ing up          or just go-ing down?          It's just a    mat-ter of time    un-til we're

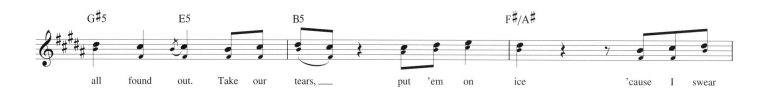

all    found    out.    Take    our    tears,          put 'em    on    ice          'cause I    swear

I'd    burn    this    cit-y    down    to    show    you    the    light.

# Champagne for My Real Friends, Real Pain for My Sham Friends

**Words and Music by Patrick Stumph, Peter Wentz, Andrew Hurley and Joseph Trohman**

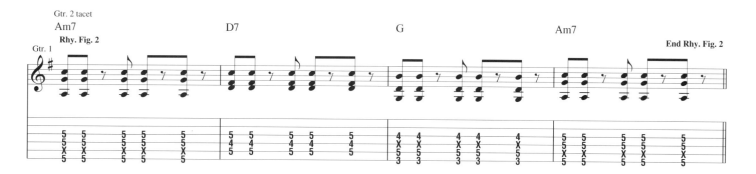

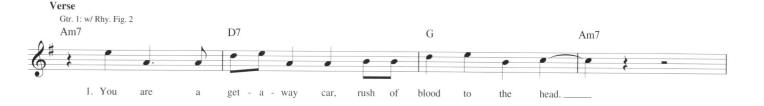

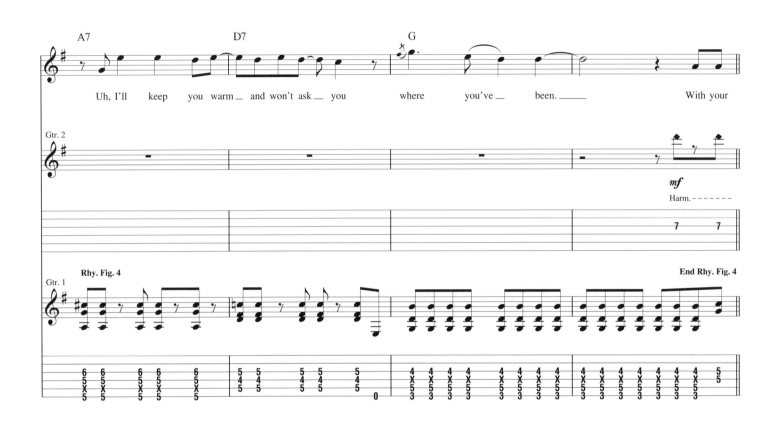

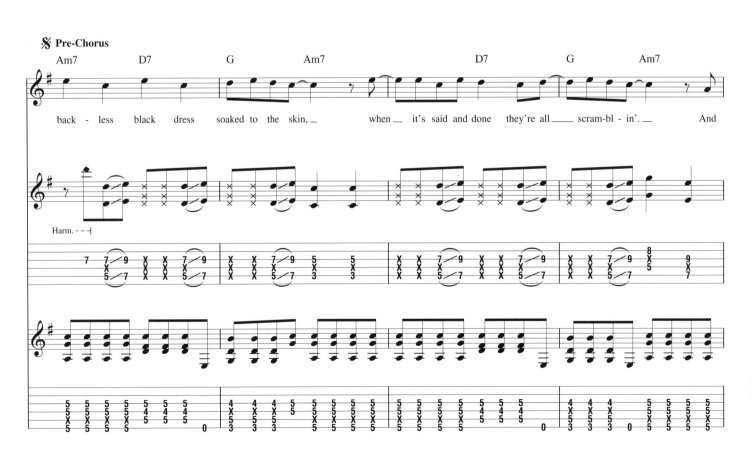

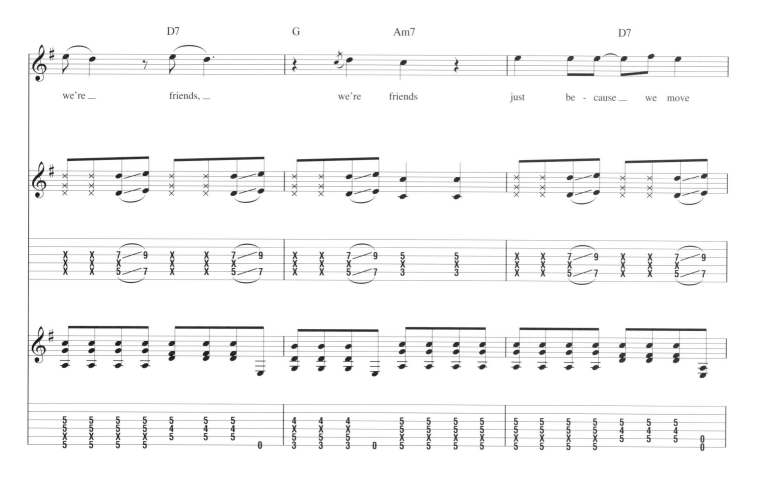

we're __ friends, __ we're friends just be - cause __ we move

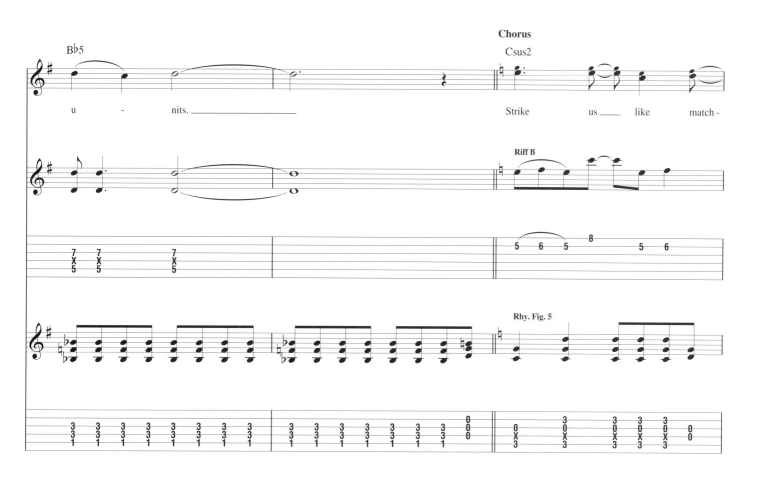

u - nits. __ Strike us __ like match-

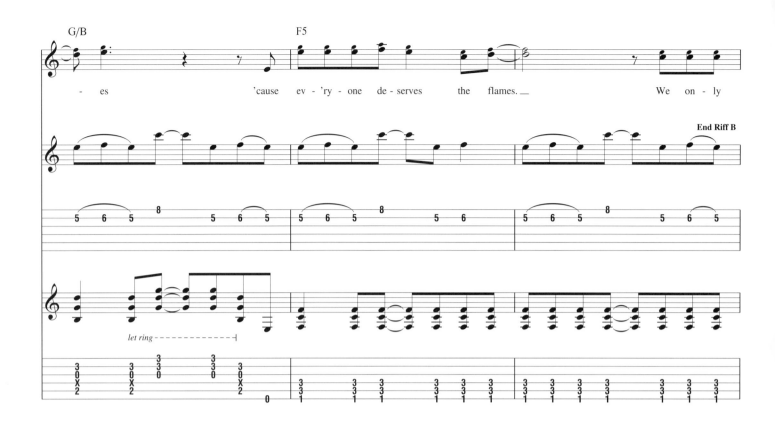

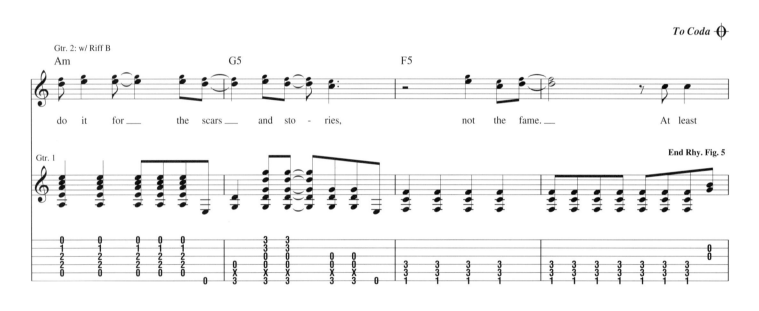

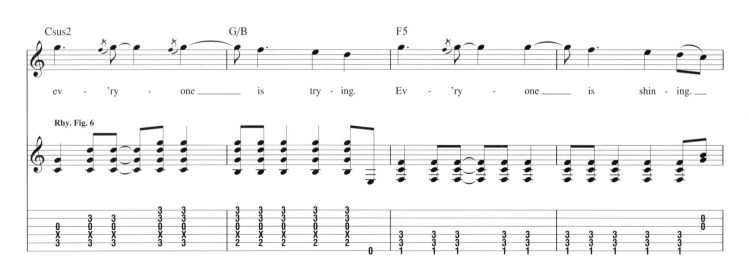

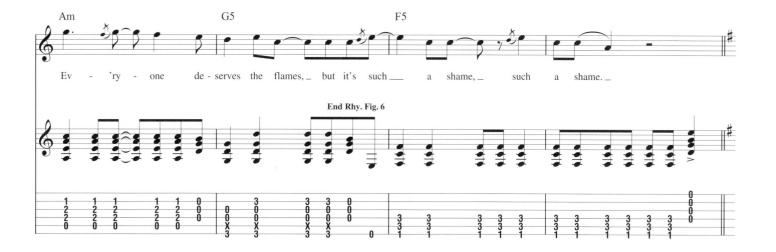

Ev-'ry-one deserves the flames, _ but it's such _ a shame, _ such a shame. _

End Rhy. Fig. 6

**Interlude**

Gtr. 1: w/ Rhy. Fig. 1 (2 times)
Gtr. 2: w/ Riff A (2 times)

D6(no3rd)    E                          D6(no3rd)    E

**Verse**

Gtr. 1: w/ Rhy. Fig. 2

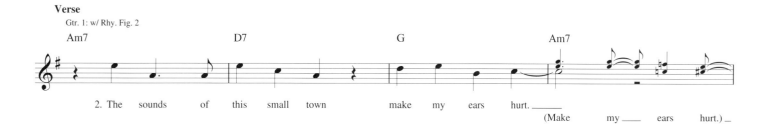

Am7                    D7                    G                    Am7

2. The sounds of this small town make my ears hurt. _

(Make my _ ears hurt.) _

Gtr. 1: w/ Rhy. Fig. 3

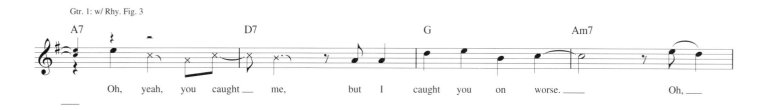

A7                    D7                    G                    Am7

Oh, yeah, you caught _ me, but I caught you on worse. _    Oh, _

Gtr. 1: w/ Rhy. Fig. 2

D7                    G                    Am7

they say... But who are you fight-ing for? Tide's _

("You want a war? You've got a war!") _

Gtr. 2

P.M.

**Coda**

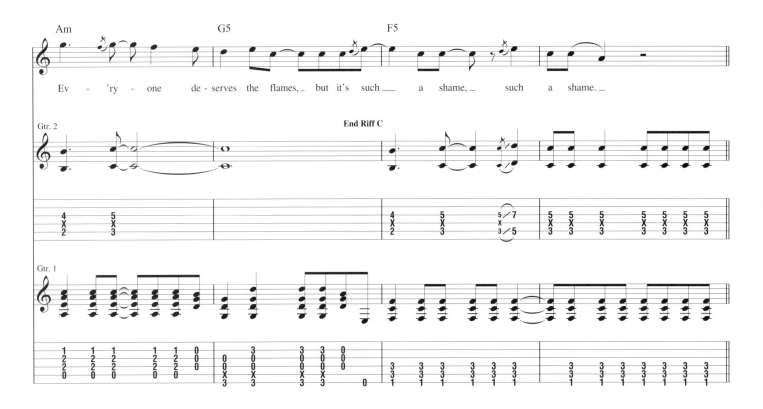

## Interlude

Gtrs. 1 & 2 tacet

*Chord symbols implied by bass, next 16 meas.     **Position vol. knob at 1/2 volume.

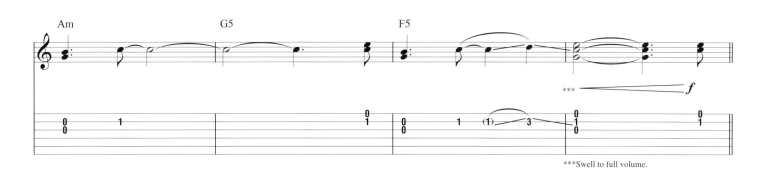

***Swell to full volume.

## Bridge

Gtr. 3 tacet

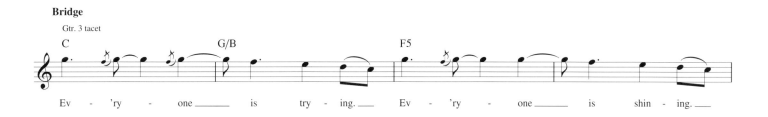

Ev - 'ry - one ___ is try - ing. ___ Ev - 'ry - one ___ is shin - ing. ___

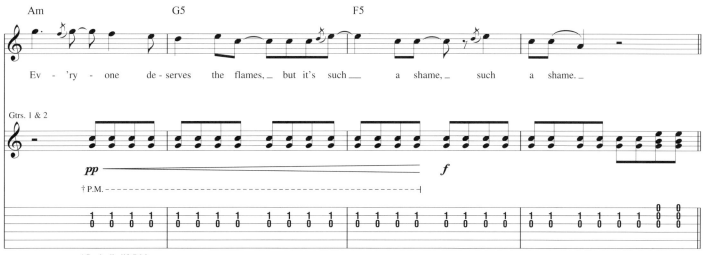

Ev - 'ry - one de - serves the flames, ___ but it's such ___ a shame, ___ such a shame. ___

Gtrs. 1 & 2

† P.M.

†Gradually lift P.M.

**Outro-Chorus**

Gtr. 1: w/ Rhy. Fig. 5
Gtr. 2: w/ Riff B (2 times)

Strike us like match - es 'cause ev - 'ry - one de - serves the flames. ___ We on - ly

do it for ___ the scars ___ and sto - ries, not the fame. ___ At least

Gtr. 1: w/ Rhy. Fig. 6
Gtr. 2: w/ Riff C

ev - 'ry - one ___ is try - ing. Ev - 'ry - one ___

___ is shin - ing. ___ Ev - 'ry - one de - serves the flames, ___ but it's

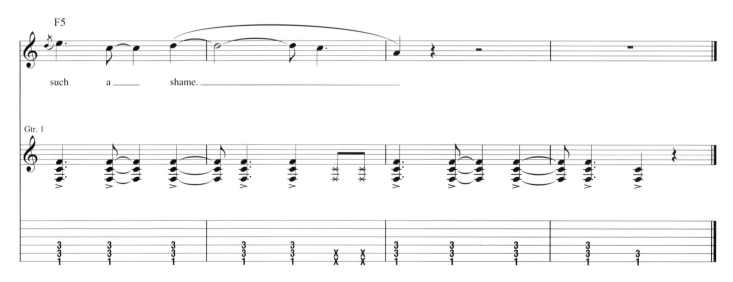

such a ___ shame. ___

Gtr. 1

# I Slept With Someone in Fall Out Boy and All I Got Was This Stupid Song Written About Me

### Words and Music by Patrick Stumph, Peter Wentz, Andrew Hurley and Joseph Trohman

Drop D tuning:
(low to high) D-A-D-G-B-E

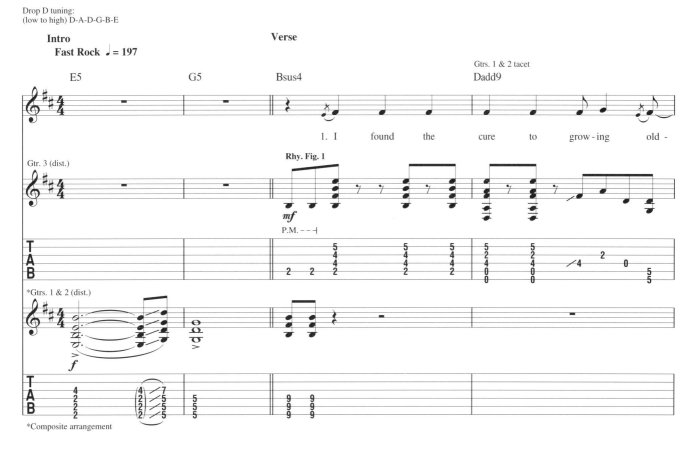

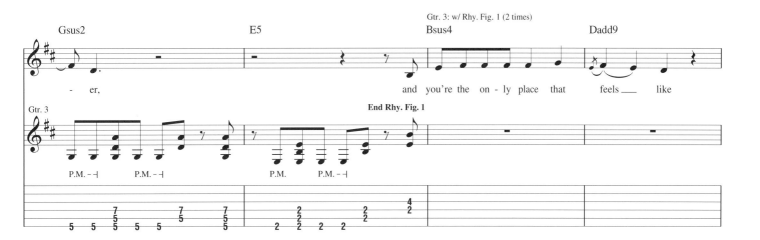

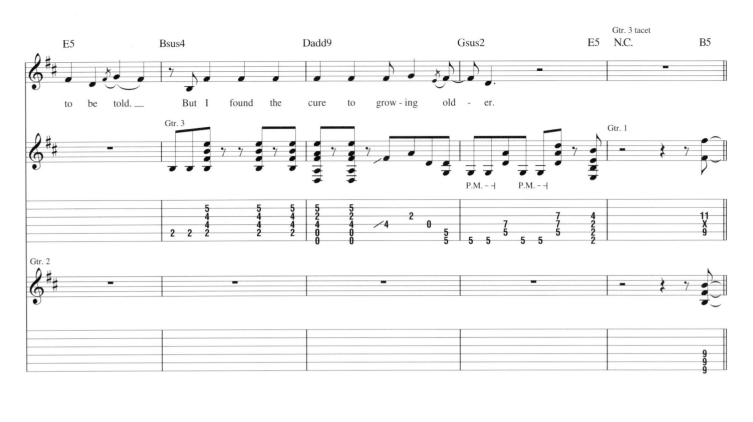

to be told. __ But I found the cure to grow-ing old - er.

Interlude

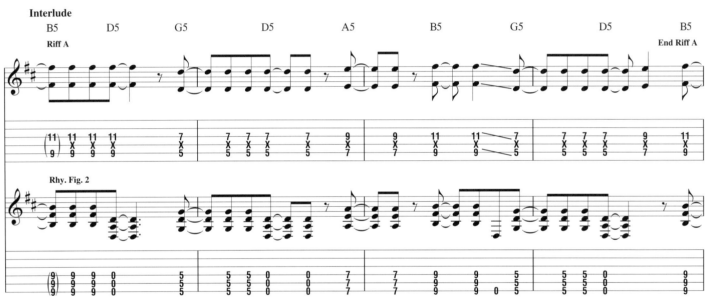

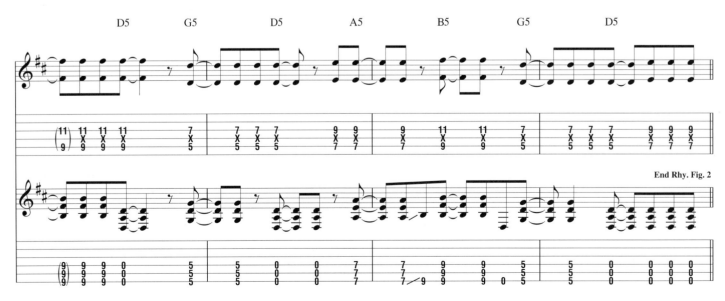

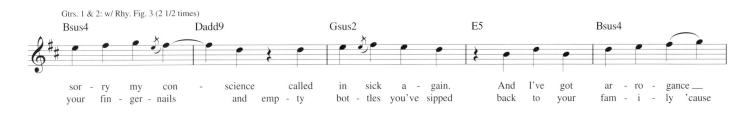

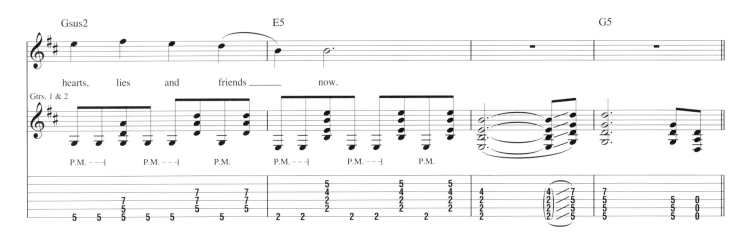

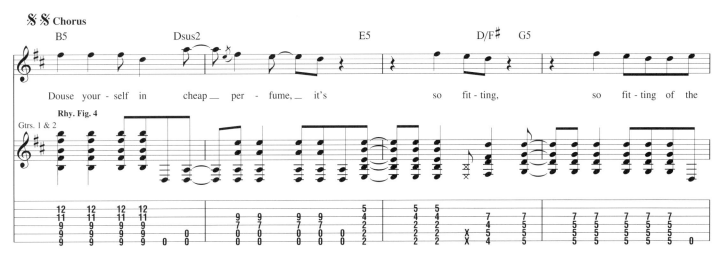

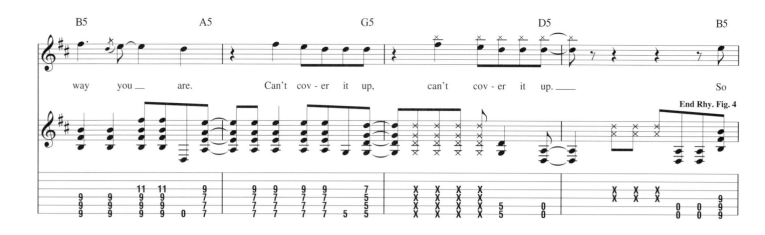

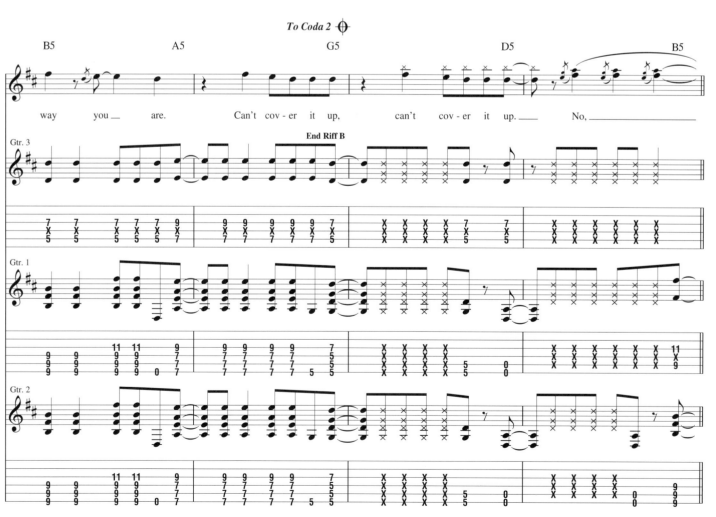

**Interlude**

Gtr. 1: w/ Riff A
Gtr. 2: w/ Rhy. Fig. 2
Gtr. 3 tacet

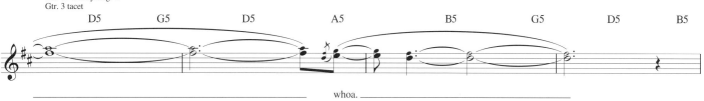

whoa.

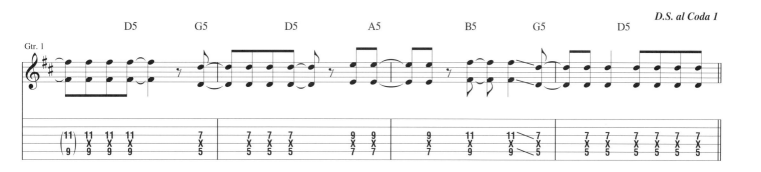

*D.S. al Coda 1*

**⊕ Coda 1**

**Half-time feel**

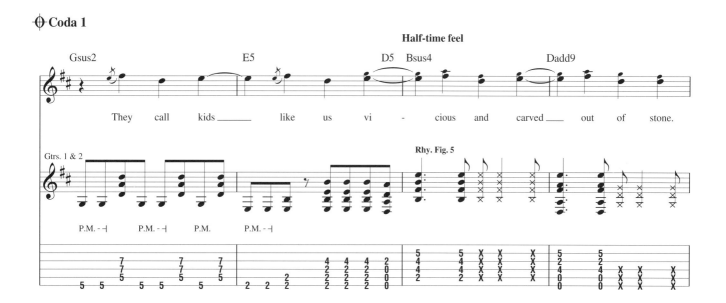

They call kids ___ like us vi - cious and carved ___ out of stone.

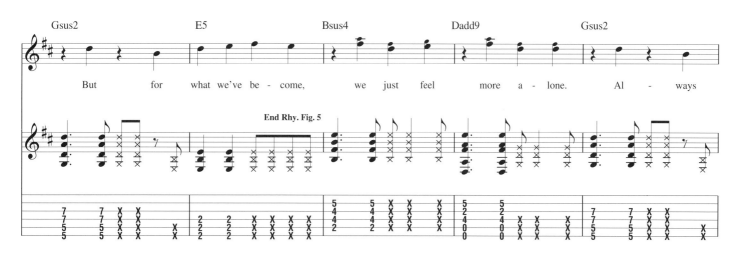

But for what we've be - come, we just feel more a - lone. Al - ways

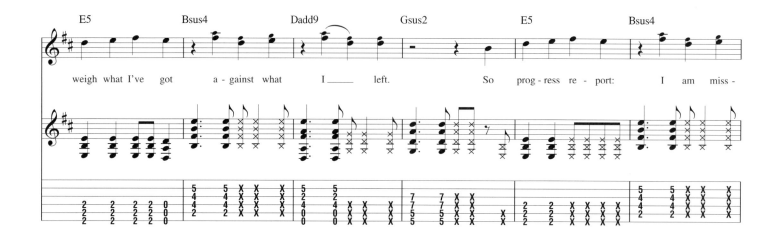

weigh what I've got a - gainst what I ___ left. So prog - ress re - port: I am miss-

*D.S.S. al Coda 2*
**End half-time feel**

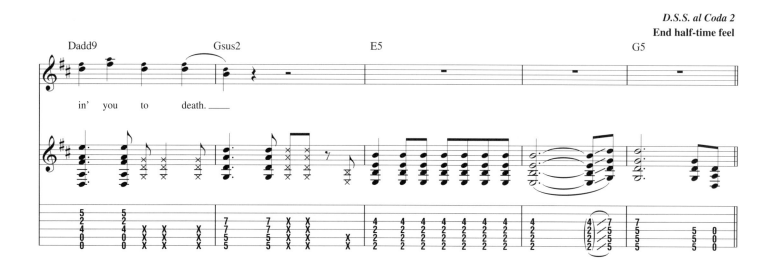

in' you to death. ___

**Coda 2**

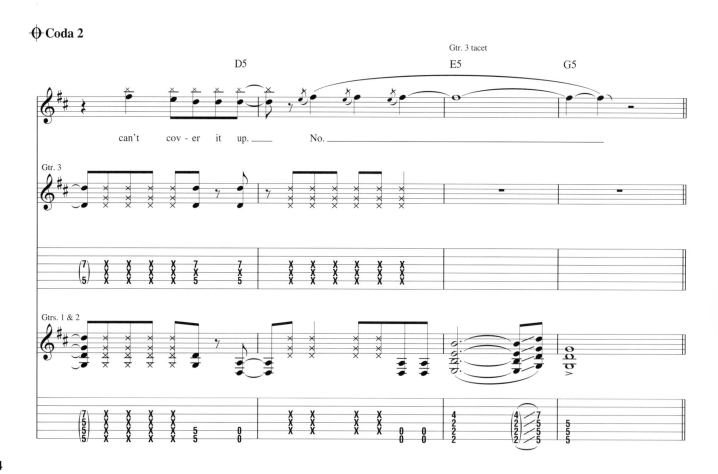

can't cov - er it up. ___ No.

Gtr. 3

Gtrs. 1 & 2

**Bridge**

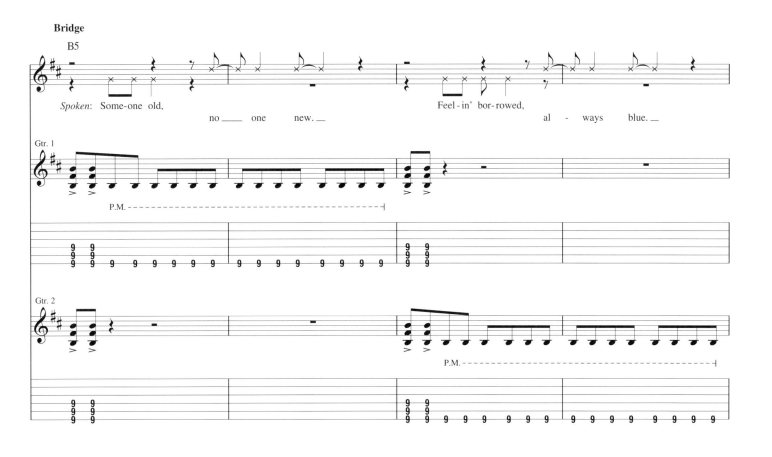

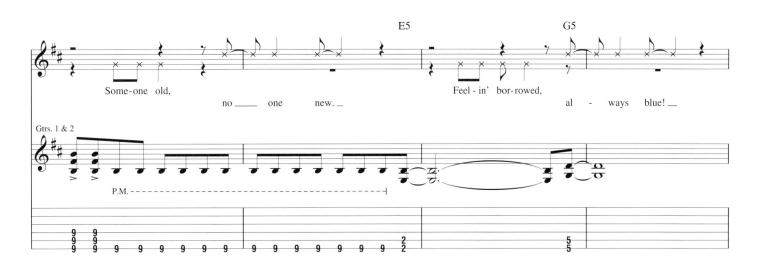

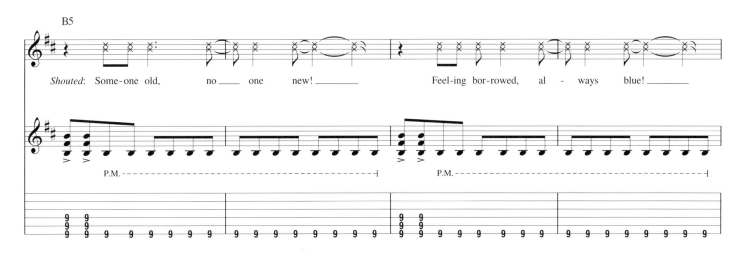

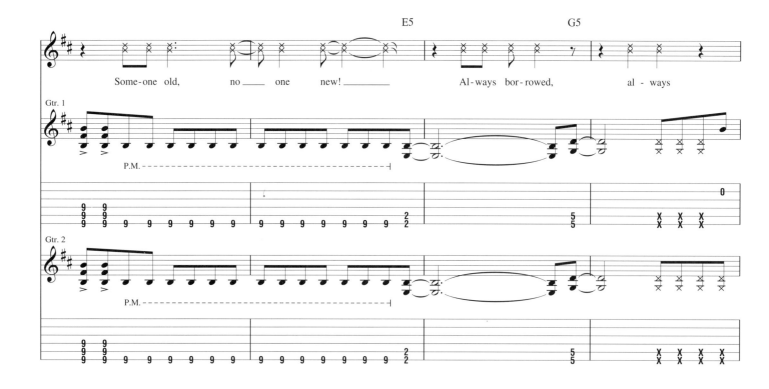

Some-one old, no _____ one new! _____ Al-ways bor-rowed, al - ways

**Half-time feel**

Gtr. 2: w/ Rhy. Fig. 5 (3 1/4 times)

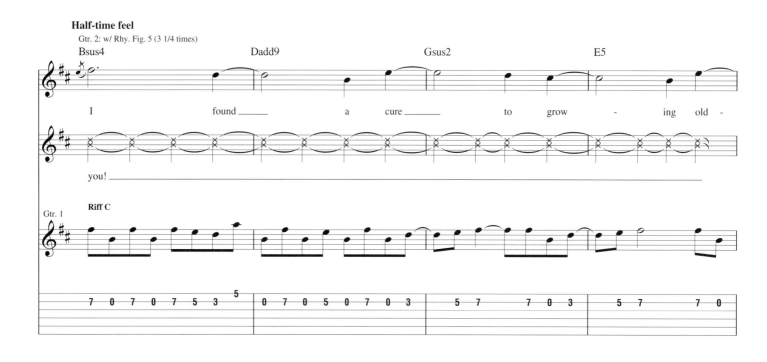

I found _____ a cure _____ to grow - ing old -

you! _____

**Riff C**

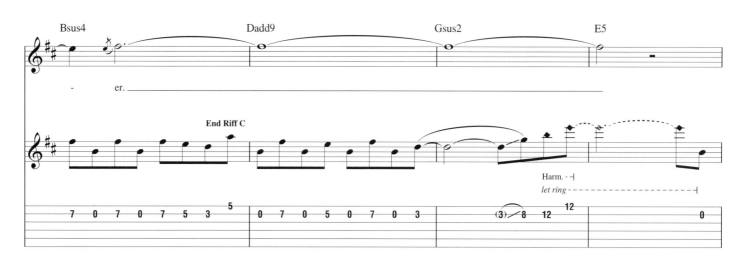

- er. _____

**End Riff C**

Harm.

*let ring*

Gtr. 1: w/ Riff C

Bsus4         Dadd9         Gsus2         E5         Bsus4

I     found _____ a    cure _____ to   grow - ing   old - er. _____

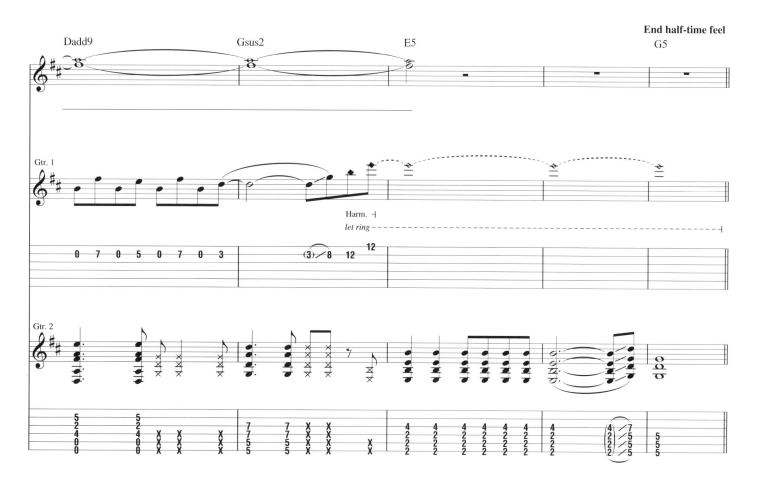

End half-time feel

Dadd9         Gsus2         E5         G5

Gtr. 1

Harm.
let ring - - - - - - - - - - - - - - - - - - - - - - - - - - - - - - - - -

Gtr. 2

## Outro-Chorus

Gtrs. 1 & 2: w/ Rhy. Fig. 4 (1 6/8 times)

B5         Dsus2         E5         D/F#    G5

Douse your - self   in   cheap ___ per - fume, _ it's       so   fit - ting,       so   fit - ting  of  the

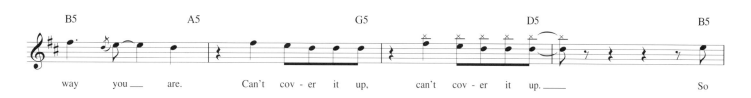

B5         A5         G5         D5         B5

way    you ___ are.   Can't  cov - er  it  up,   can't  cov - er  it  up. ___       So

Gtr. 3: w/ Riff B

douse your - self in cheap ____ per - fume, ____ it's        so     fit - ting,

so     fit - ting of the way    you ____ are.     Can't  cov - er   it   up,

can't cov - er  it  up! ____

Gtr. 2

*p ————————————— f
fdbk.

*Vol. swell                    Pitch: E♭

Gtr. 1

8va - - - - - - - - - - - - - - - - - - -

***mp ——— f
**fdbk.

Pitch: B        G
**Microphonic fdbk., not caused by string vibration.
***Vol. swell

Gtr. 3

# A Little Less Sixteen Candles, a Little More "Touch Me"

Words and Music by Patrick Stumph, Peter Wentz, Andrew Hurley and Joseph Trohman

Drop D tuning:
(low to high) D-A-D-G-B-E

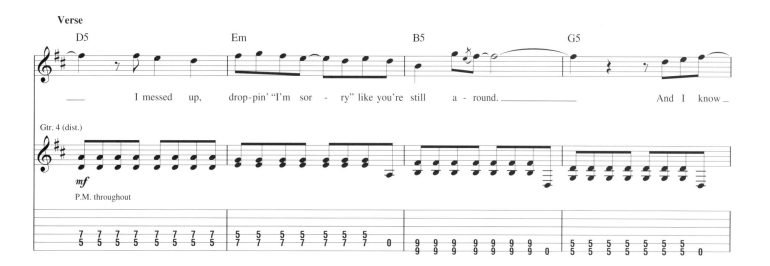

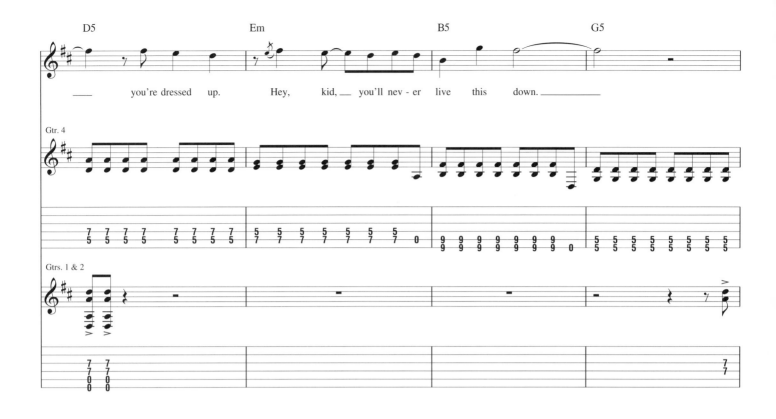

___ you're dressed up. Hey, kid, ___ you'll nev - er live this down. ___

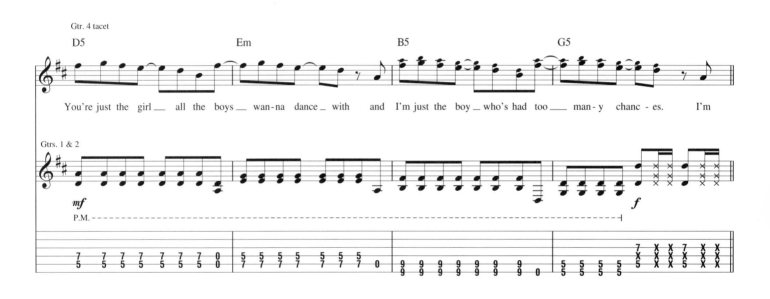

You're just the girl ___ all the boys ___ wan-na dance ___ with    and I'm just the boy ___ who's had too ___ man - y chanc - es.    I'm

**Pre-Chorus**

sleep-in' on your folks' porch ___ a - gain, dream-in'. She said, she said, ___ she said, "Why don't you just ___ drop dead?"

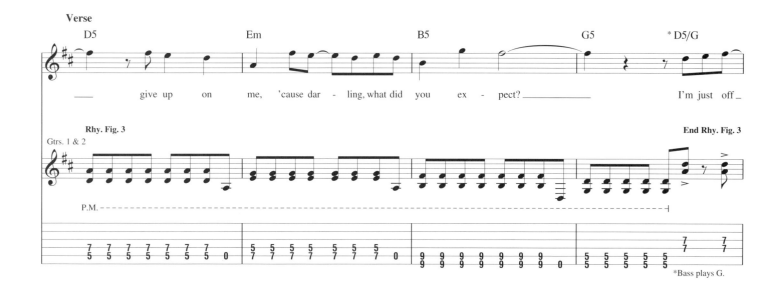

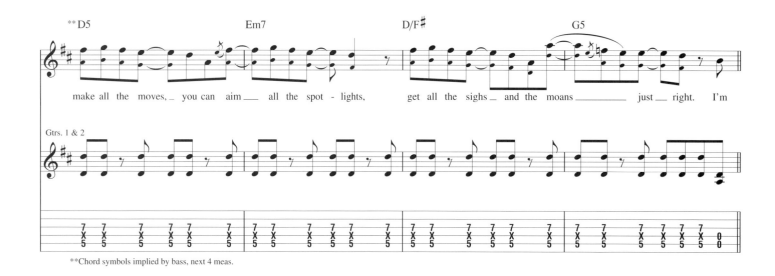

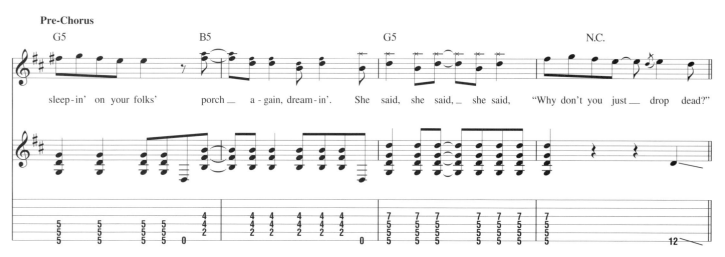

**Chorus**

I don't blame you __ for __ be-ing you, __ but you can't blame __ me for hat-ing it. __ So

say, what are you wait-ing for? Kiss her, kiss her. __ I set my clocks ear-ly 'cause I know I'm al-ways late. __

**Bridge**

**Half-time feel**

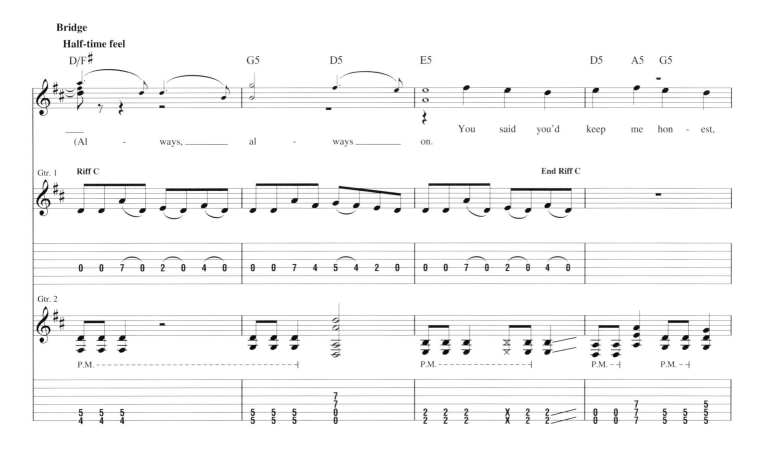

(Al - ways, __ al - ways __ on.  You said you'd keep me hon - est,

Gtr. 1  **Riff C** ... **End Riff C**

Gtr. 2  P.M.

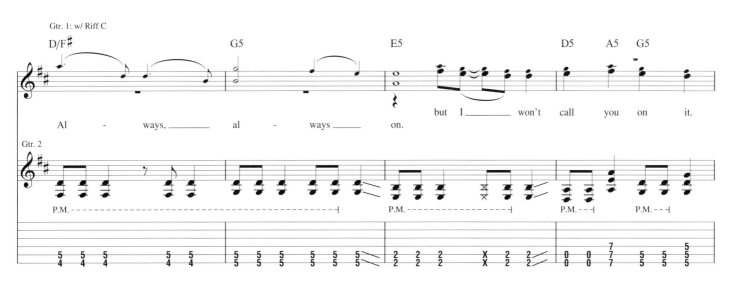

Gtr. 1: w/ Riff C

Al - ways, __ al - ways __ on.  but I __ won't call you on it.

Gtr. 2

**Chorus**
Gtrs. 1 & 2: w/ Rhy. Fig. 2 (2 times)
Gtr. 5: w/ Riff B (2 times)

I don't blame you __ for __ be - ing you, __ but you can't blame __ me for hat - ing it. __ So

say, what are you wait - ing for? Kiss her, kiss her. __ I set my clocks ear - ly 'cause I know I'm al - ways late.

**Outro**
Gtrs. 1 & 2: w/ Rhy. Fig. 1 (1 1/4 times)
Gtr. 3: w/ Riff A (1 1/4 times)

I set my clocks ear - ly 'cause I know I'm al - ways late. __

# Get Busy Living or Get Busy Dying
## (Do Your Part to Save the Scene and Stop Going to Shows)

Words and Music by Patrick Stumph, Peter Wentz, Andrew Hurley and Joseph Trohman

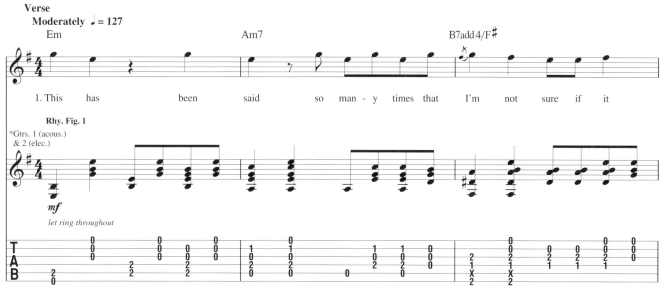

*Gtr. 2 w/ slight dist. Composite arrangement

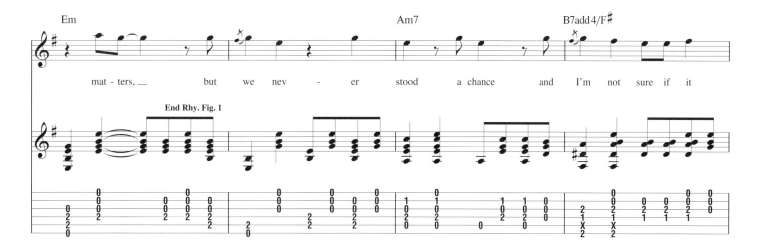

**Doubled throughout

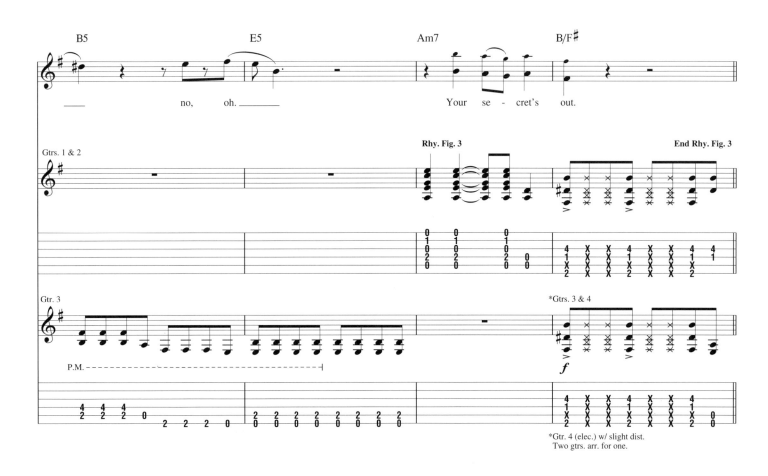

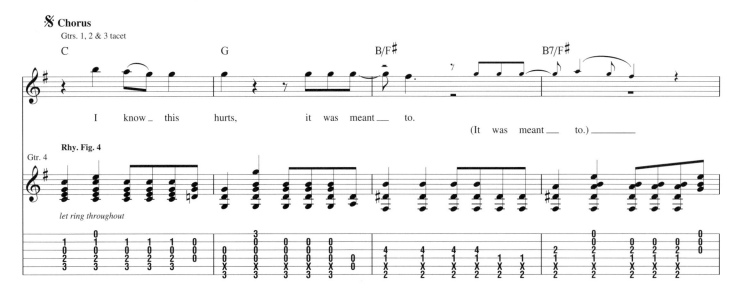

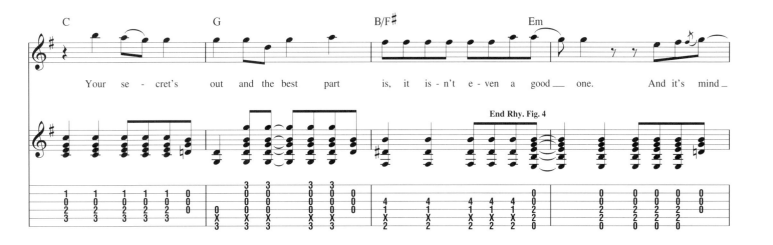

Your se- cret's out and the best part is, it is- n't e- ven a good __ one. And it's mind __

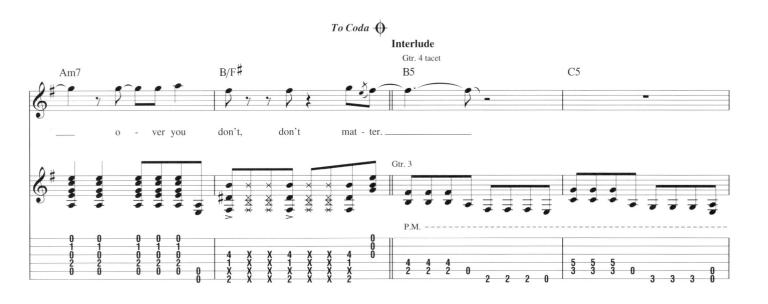

*To Coda* ⊕

**Interlude**

Gtr. 4 tacet

__ o- ver you don't, don't mat- ter. _____

Gtr. 3

P.M. - - - - - - - - - - - - - - - - - - - - - - - - - - - - - - - - - -

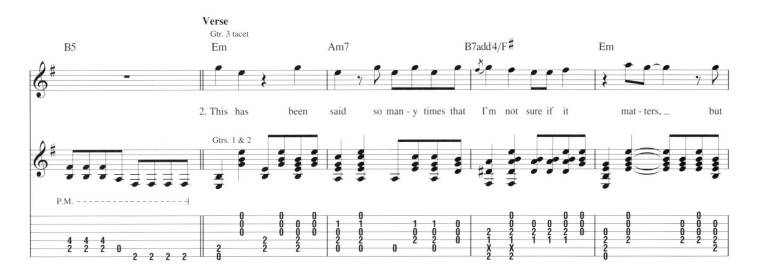

**Verse**

Gtr. 3 tacet

2. This has been said so man- y times that I'm not sure if it mat- ters, __ but

Gtrs. 1 & 2

P.M. - - - - - - - - - - - - - - - - |

Gtrs. 1 & 2: w/ Rhy. Fig. 1

Gtr. 3: w/ Rhy. Fig. 2

it must be said a- gain that all us boys are just scream- ing __ in- to mi-

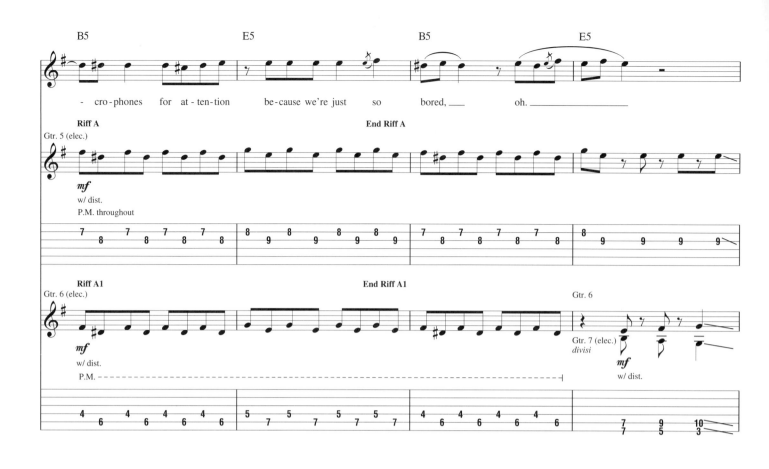

- cro-phones for at-ten-tion be-cause we're just so bored, ___ oh. ___

**Riff A**

Gtr. 5 (elec.)

*mf*

w/ dist.
P.M. throughout

**End Riff A**

**Riff A1**

Gtr. 6 (elec.)

*mf*

w/ dist.
P.M. - - - - - - - - - - - - - - - - - - - - - - - - - - - - - - - - - - - - - - - - - - - - - - - |

**End Riff A1**

Gtr. 6

Gtr. 7 (elec.)
*divisi*

*mf*
w/ dist.

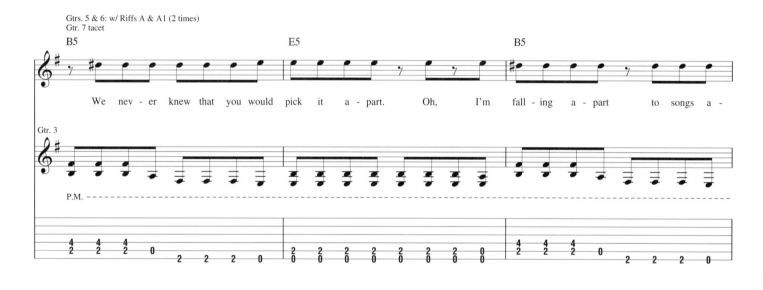

Gtrs. 5 & 6: w/ Riffs A & A1 (2 times)
Gtr. 7 tacet

We nev-er knew that you would pick it a-part. Oh, I'm fall-ing a-part to songs a-

Gtr. 3

P.M. - - - - - - - - - - - - - - - - - - - - - - - - - - - - - - - - - - - - - - - - - - - - - - - - - - - - - - - - -

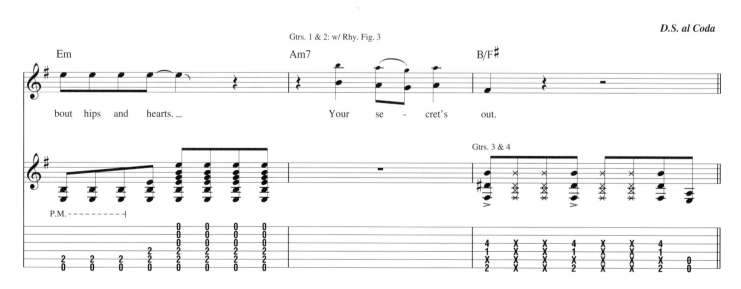

*D.S. al Coda*

Gtrs. 1 & 2: w/ Rhy. Fig. 3

Em                          Am7                          B/F#

bout hips and hearts. ___          Your se - cret's out.

Gtrs. 3 & 4

P.M. - - - - |

108

## ⊕ Coda
### Bridge

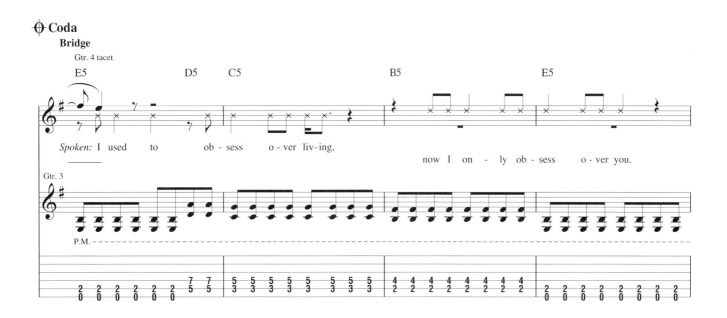

Spoken: I used to ob-sess o-ver liv-ing, now I on-ly ob-sess o-ver you.

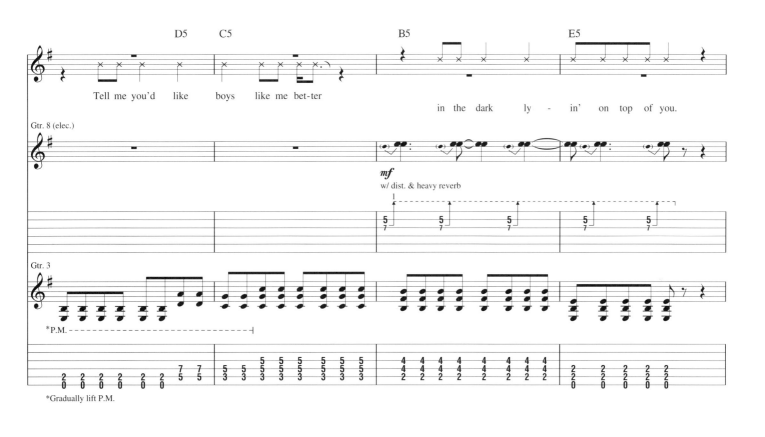

Tell me you'd like boys like me bet-ter in the dark ly-in' on top of you.

mf
w/ dist. & heavy reverb

*Gradually lift P.M.

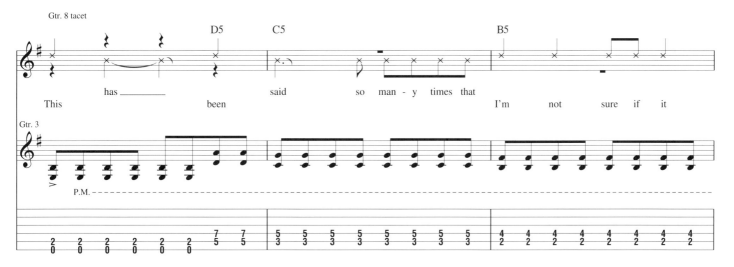

This has _____ been said so man-y times that I'm not sure if it

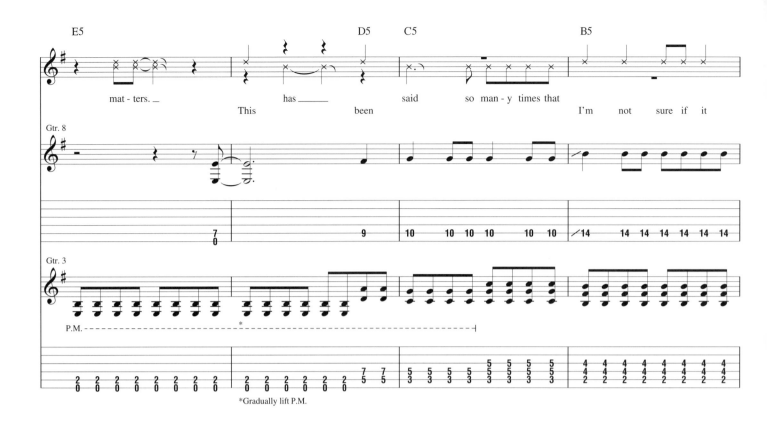

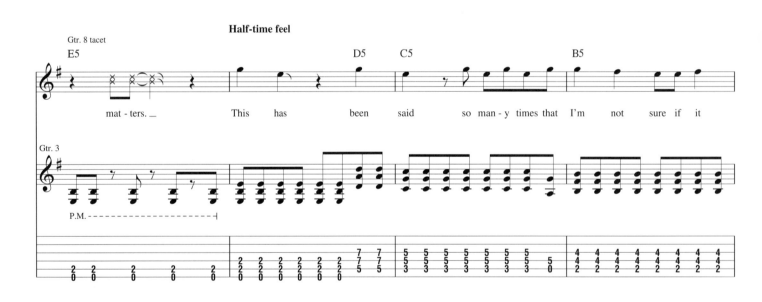

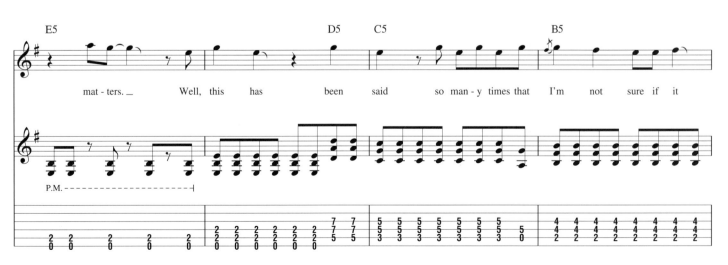

**Chorus**

**End half-time feel**

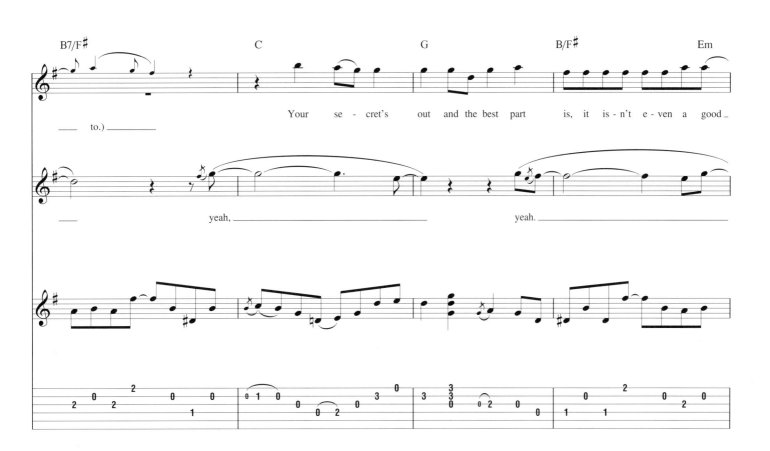

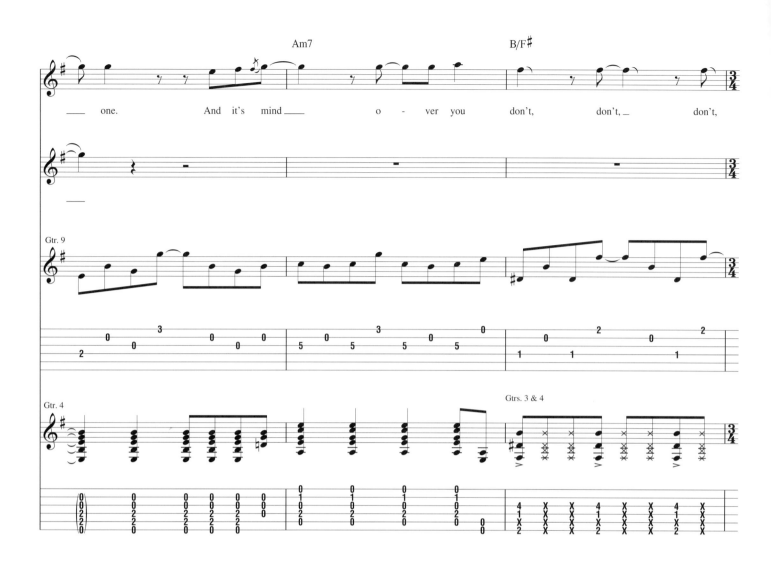

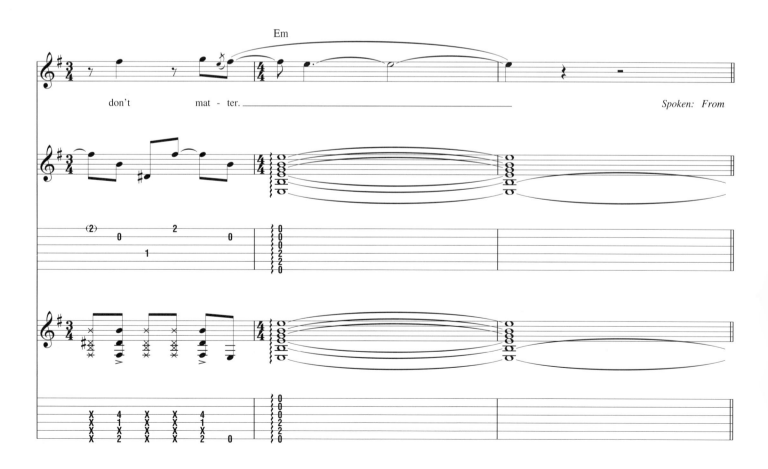

**Outro**
**Free time**

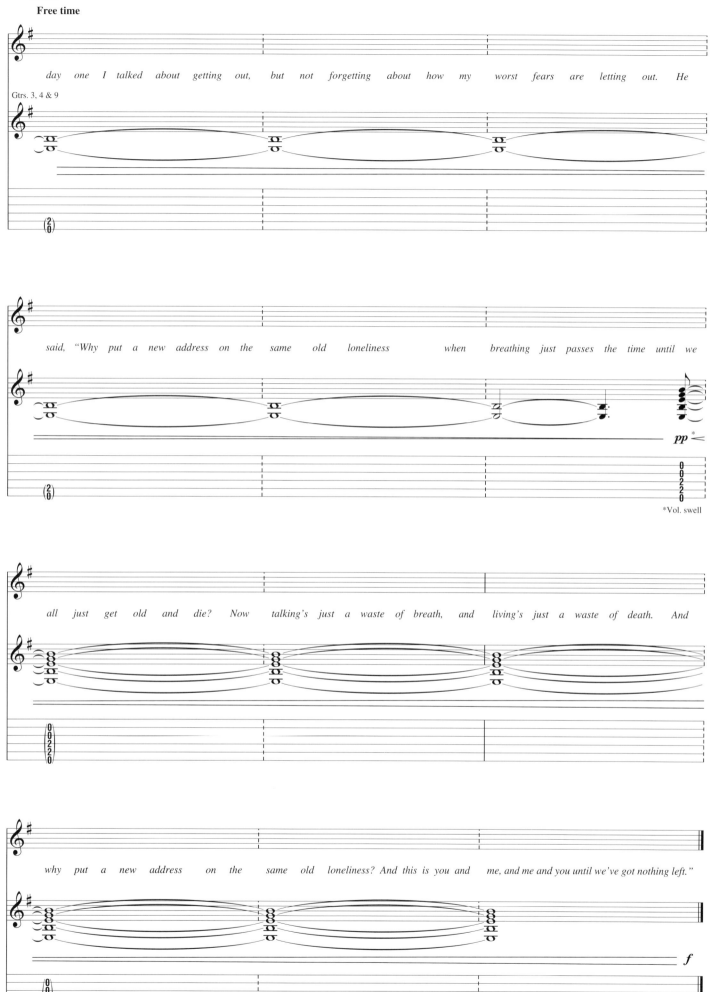

day one I talked about getting out, but not forgetting about how my worst fears are letting out. He

Gtrs. 3, 4 & 9

said, "Why put a new address on the same old loneliness when breathing just passes the time until we

*pp*

*Vol. swell

all just get old and die? Now talking's just a waste of breath, and living's just a waste of death. And

why put a new address on the same old loneliness? And this is you and me, and me and you until we've got nothing left."

*f*

# XO

**Words and Music by Patrick Stumph, Peter Wentz, Andrew Hurley and Joseph Trohman**

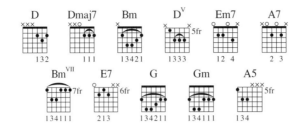

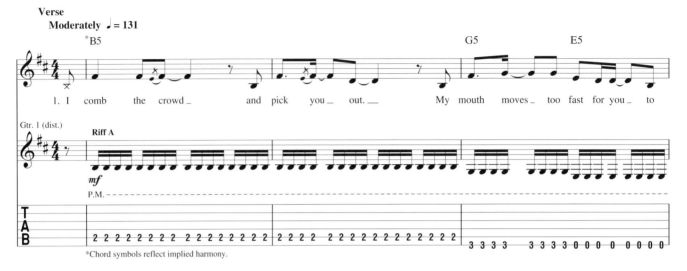

*Chord symbols reflect implied harmony.

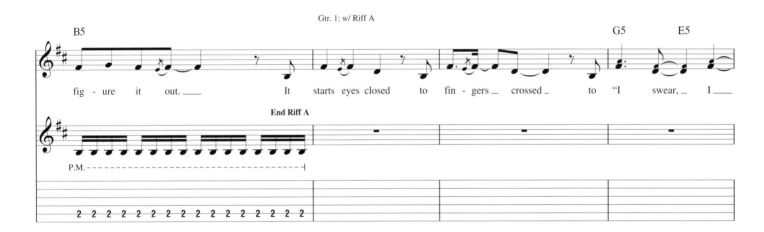

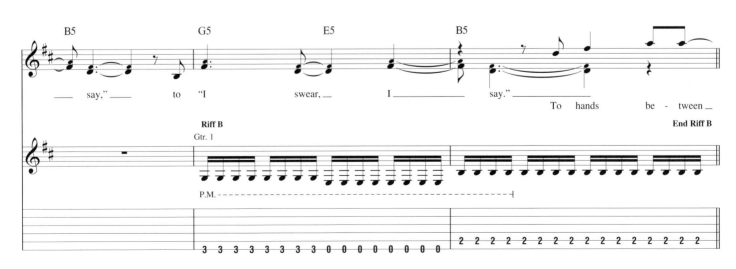

**Pre-Chorus**
**Double-time feel**

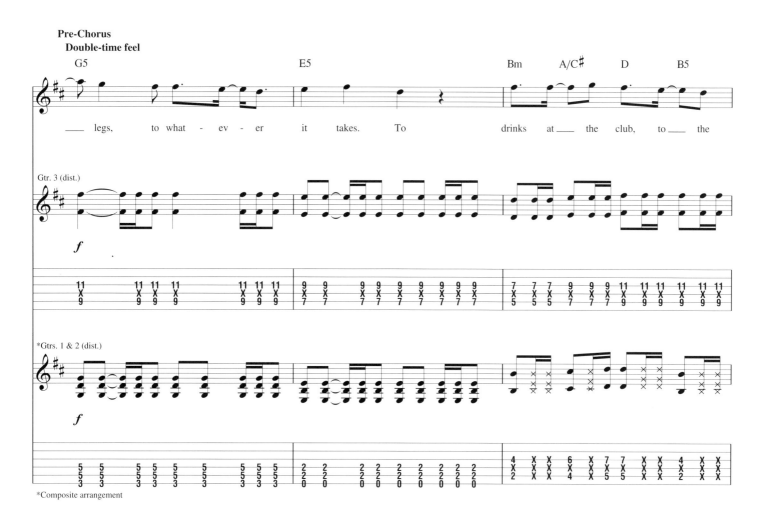

*Composite arrangement

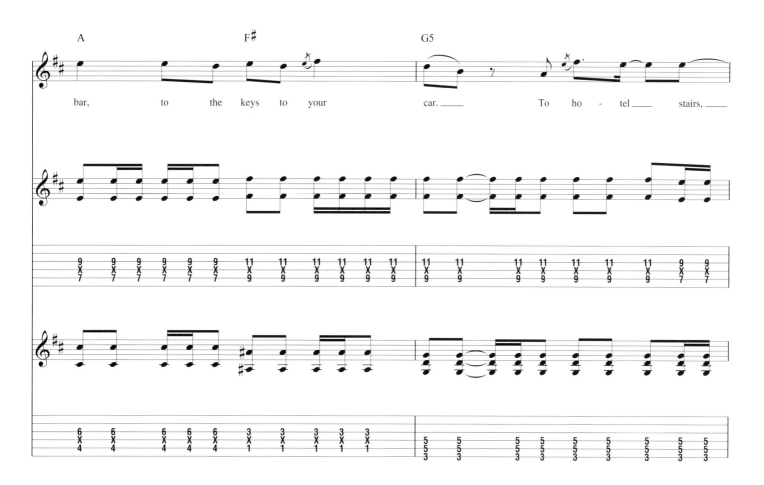

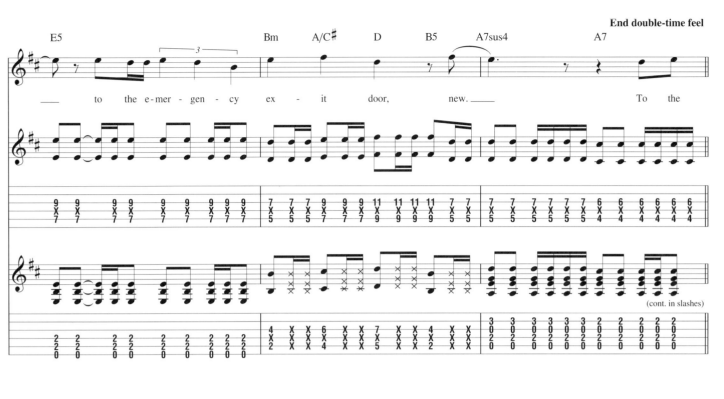

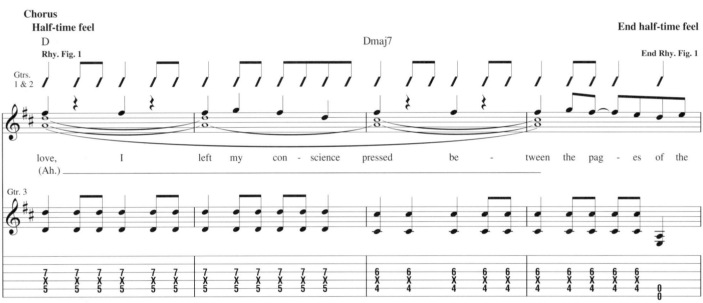

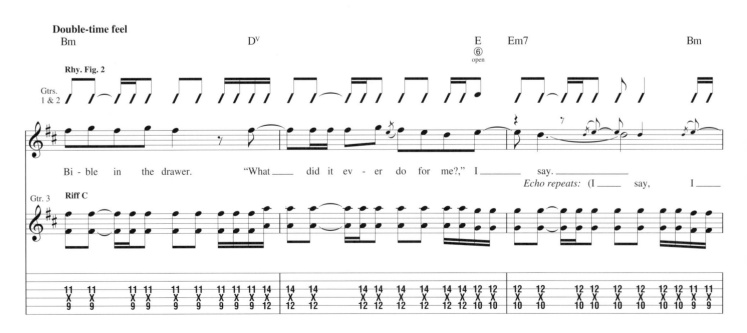

116

**Verse**

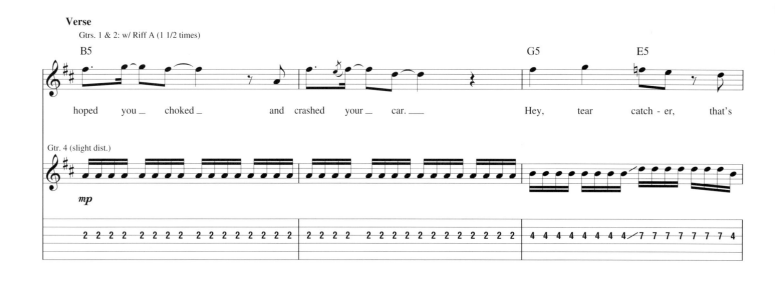

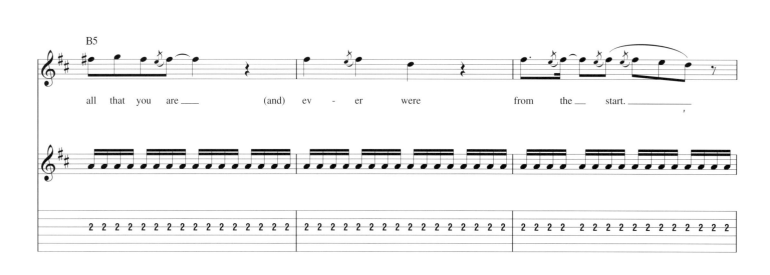

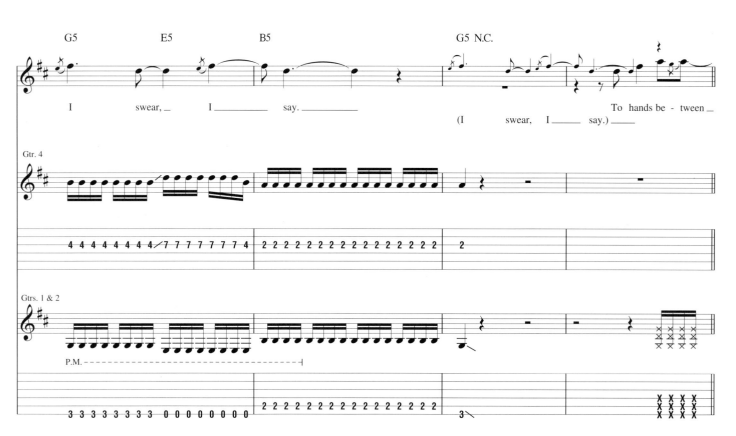

**Pre-Chorus**
**Double-time feel**

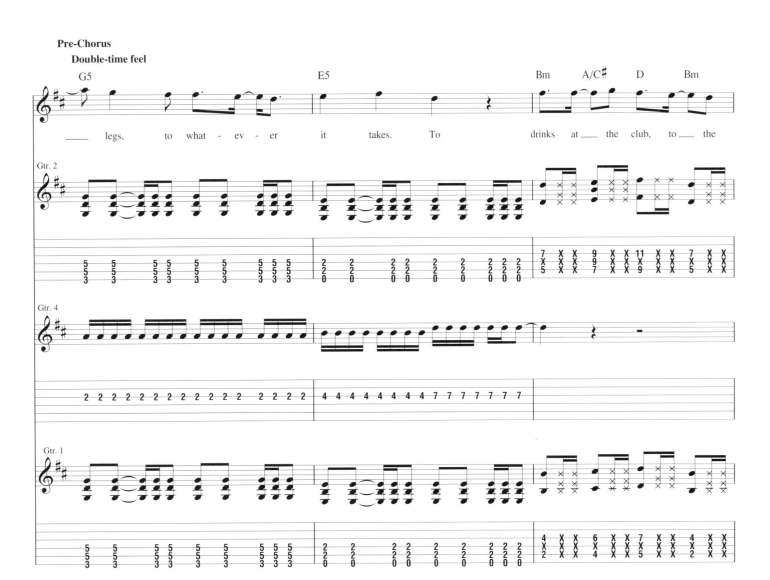

legs, to what - ev - er it takes. To drinks at ___ the club, to ___ the

bar, to the keys to your car. ___ To ho - tel ___ stairs, in - to the e - mer - gen - cy

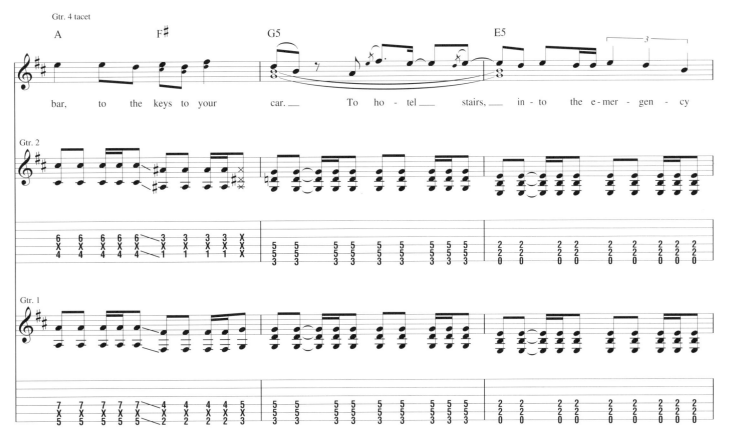

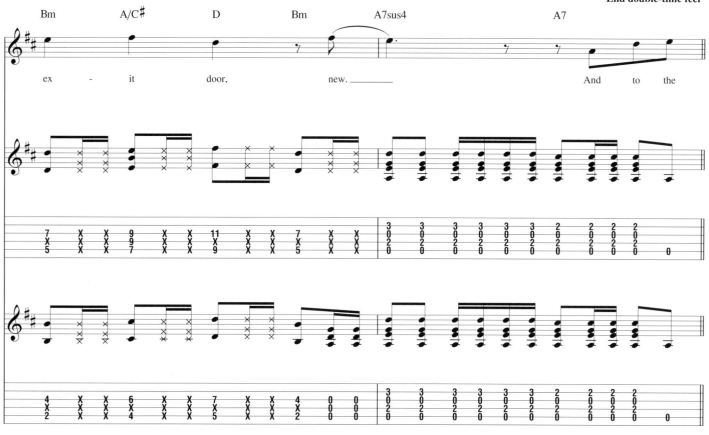

ex - it door, new._____ And to the

**Chorus**
**Half-time feel**                                                                                            **End half-time feel**

Gtrs. 1 & 2: w/ Rhy. Fig. 1

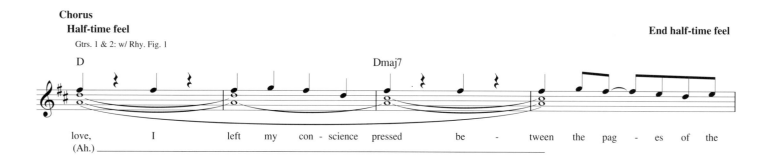

love,     I     left my con-science pressed     be - tween the pag - es of the
(Ah.) _____

**Double-time feel**

Gtrs. 1 & 2: w/ Rhy. Fig. 2 (2 times)
Gtr. 3: w/ Riff C (2 times)

Bi - ble in the drawer. "What__ did it ev - er do for me?," I_____ say._____
*Echo repeats:* (I___ say,   I___ say,   I___ say.)

Gtrs. 1 & 2: w/ Rhy. Fig. 3
Gtr. 3: w/ Riff D

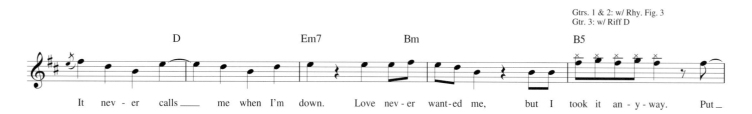

It nev - er calls___ me when I'm down.  Love nev - er want-ed me,  but I took it an - y-way. Put__

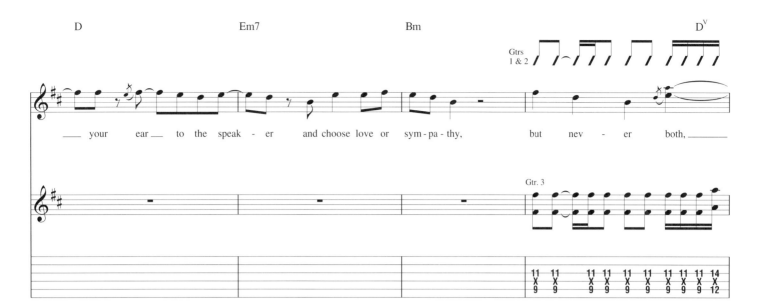

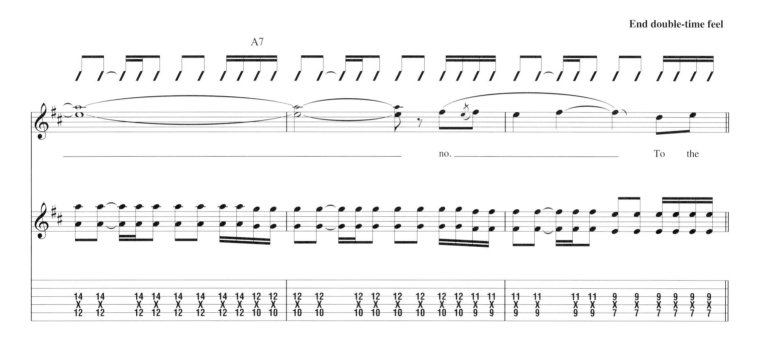

**End double-time feel**

**Bridge**
**Half-time feel**

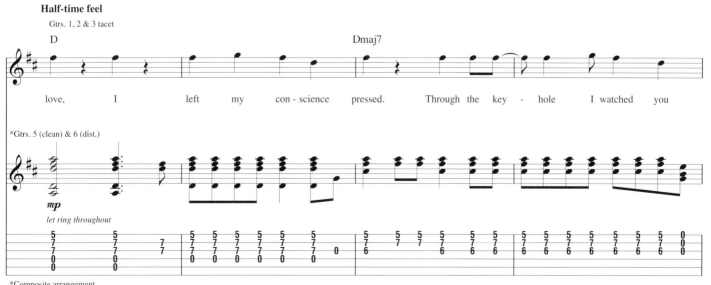

*Composite arrangement

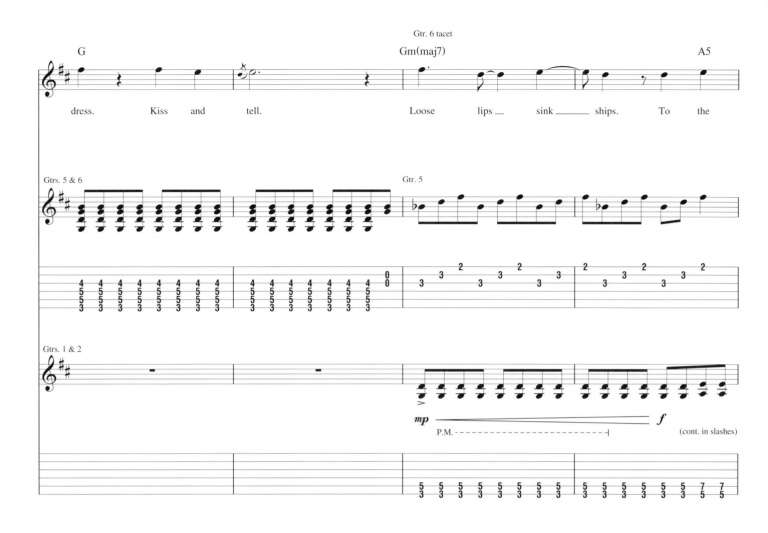

dress.    Kiss    and    tell.                Loose    lips ___ sink _____ ships.    To    the

love,            I        left    my    con - science    pressed.    Through    the    key - holes    I    watched    you

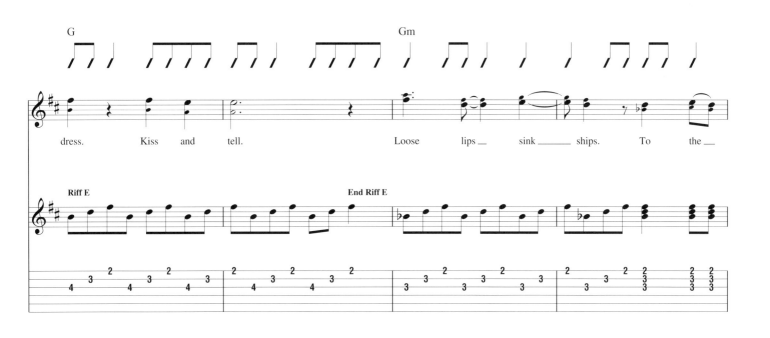

dress. Kiss and tell. Loose lips __ sink _____ ships. To the __

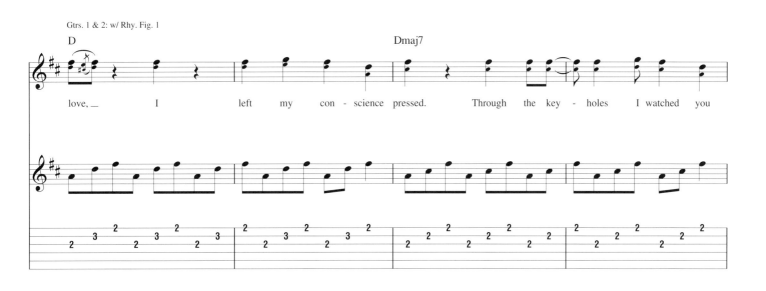

love, __ I left my con - science pressed. Through the key - holes I watched you

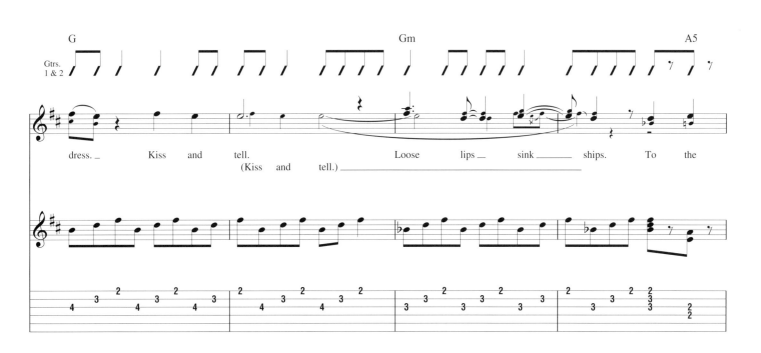

dress. __ Kiss and tell. Loose lips __ sink _____ ships. To the
(Kiss and tell.) _____

Gtrs. 1 & 2: w/ Rhy. Fig. 4 (3 times)
Gtr. 5: w/ Riff E (6 times)

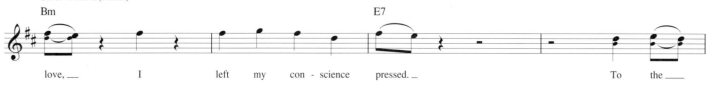

love, __ I left my con - science pressed. __ To the __

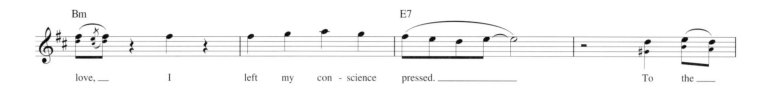

love, __ I left my con - science pressed. _____ To the __

love, I left my con - science pressed be - tween the pag - es of the

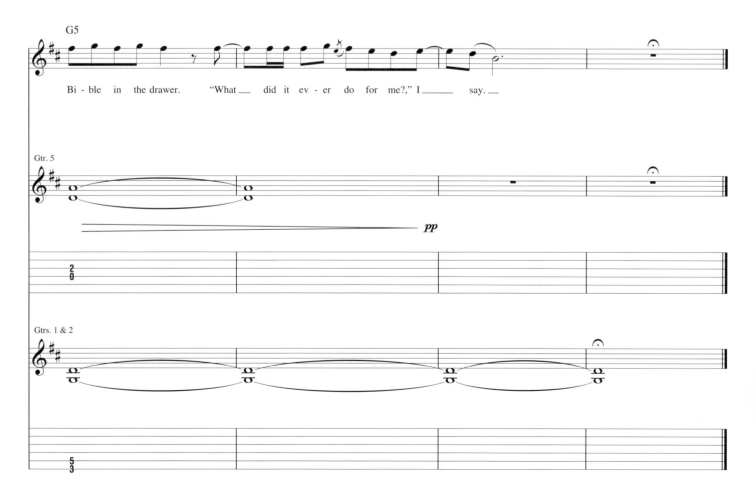

Bi - ble in the drawer. "What __ did it ev - er do for me?," I _____ say. __

Gtr. 5

pp

Gtrs. 1 & 2

124

# Guitar Notation Legend

Guitar Music can be notated three different ways: on a *musical staff*, in *tablature*, and in *rhythm slashes*.

**RHYTHM SLASHES** are written above the staff. Strum chords in the rhythm indicated. Use the chord diagrams found at the top of the first page of the transcription for the appropriate chord voicings. Round noteheads indicate single notes.

**THE MUSICAL STAFF** shows pitches and rhythms and is divided by bar lines into measures. Pitches are named after the first seven letters of the alphabet.

**TABLATURE** graphically represents the guitar fingerboard. Each horizontal line represents a a string, and each number represents a fret.

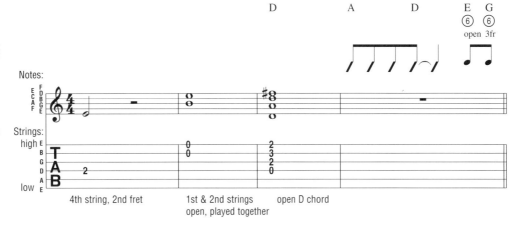

# Definitions for Special Guitar Notation

**HALF-STEP BEND:** Strike the note and bend up 1/2 step.

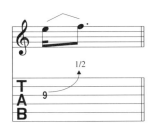

**WHOLE-STEP BEND:** Strike the note and bend up one step.

**GRACE NOTE BEND:** Strike the note and immediately bend up as indicated.

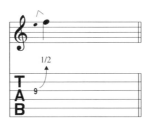

**SLIGHT (MICROTONE) BEND:** Strike the note and bend up 1/4 step.

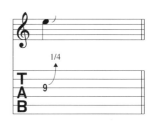

**BEND AND RELEASE:** Strike the note and bend up as indicated, then release back to the original note. Only the first note is struck.

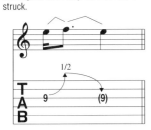

**PRE-BEND:** Bend the note as indicated, then strike it.

**PRE-BEND AND RELEASE:** Bend the note as indicated. Strike it and release the bend back to the original note.

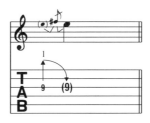

**UNISON BEND:** Strike the two notes simultaneously and bend the lower note up to the pitch of the higher.

**VIBRATO:** The string is vibrated by rapidly bending and releasing the note with the fretting hand.

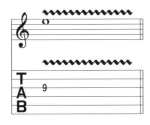

**WIDE VIBRATO:** The pitch is varied to a greater degree by vibrating with the fretting hand.

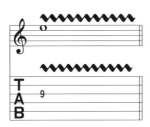

**HAMMER-ON:** Strike the first (lower) note with one finger, then sound the higher note (on the same string) with another finger by fretting it without picking.

**PULL-OFF:** Place both fingers on the notes to be sounded. Strike the first note and without picking, pull the finger off to sound the second (lower) note.

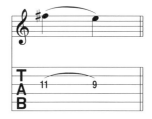

**LEGATO SLIDE:** Strike the first note and then slide the same fret-hand finger up or down to the second note. The second note is not struck.

**SHIFT SLIDE:** Same as legato slide, except the second note is struck.

**TRILL:** Very rapidly alternate between the notes indicated by continuously hammering on and pulling off.

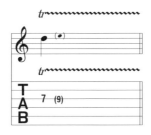

**TAPPING:** Hammer ("tap") the fret indicated with the pick-hand index or middle finger and pull off to the note fretted by the fret hand.

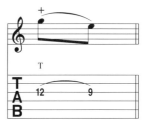

**NATURAL HARMONIC:** Strike the note while the fret-hand lightly touches the string directly over the fret indicated.

**PINCH HARMONIC:** The note is fretted normally and a harmonic is produced by adding the edge of the thumb or the tip of the index finger of the pick hand to the normal pick attack.

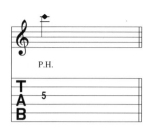

**HARP HARMONIC:** The note is fretted normally and a harmonic is produced by gently resting the pick hand's index finger directly above the indicated fret (in parentheses) while the pick hand's thumb or pick assists by plucking the appropriate string.

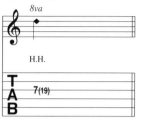

**PICK SCRAPE:** The edge of the pick is rubbed down (or up) the string, producing a scratchy sound.

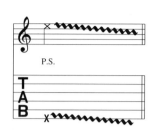

**MUFFLED STRINGS:** A percussive sound is produced by laying the fret hand across the string(s) without depressing, and striking them with the pick hand.

**PALM MUTING:** The note is partially muted by the pick hand lightly touching the string(s) just before the bridge.

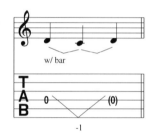

**RAKE:** Drag the pick across the strings indicated with a single motion.

**TREMOLO PICKING:** The note is picked as rapidly and continuously as possible.

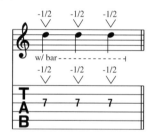

**ARPEGGIATE:** Play the notes of the chord indicated by quickly rolling them from bottom to top.

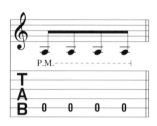

**VIBRATO BAR DIVE AND RETURN:** The pitch of the note or chord is dropped a specified number of steps (in rhythm) then returned to the original pitch.

**VIBRATO BAR SCOOP:** Depress the bar just before striking the note, then quickly release the bar.

**VIBRATO BAR DIP:** Strike the note and then immediately drop a specified number of steps, then release back to the original pitch.

# Additional Musical Definitions

| | | |
|---|---|---|
|  | *(accent)* | • Accentuate note (play it louder) |
|  | *(accent)* | • Accentuate note with great intensity |
|  | *(staccato)* | • Play the note short |
| | | • Downstroke |
| V | | • Upstroke |
| ***D.S. al Coda*** | | • Go back to the sign ( 𝄋 ), then play until the measure marked "*To Coda*," then skip to the section labelled "**Coda.**" |
| ***D.C. al Fine*** | | • Go back to the beginning of the song and play until the measure marked "***Fine***" (end). |

| | |
|---|---|
| **Rhy. Fig.** | • Label used to recall a recurring accompaniment pattern (usually chordal). |
| **Riff** | • Label used to recall composed, melodic lines (usually single notes) which recur. |
| **Fill** | • Label used to identify a brief melodic figure which is to be inserted into the arrangement. |
| **Rhy. Fill** | • A chordal version of a Fill. |
| tacet | • Instrument is silent (drops out). |
|  | • Repeat measures between signs. |
|  | • When a repeated section has different endings, play the first ending only the first time and the second ending only the second time. |

**NOTE:** Tablature numbers in parentheses mean:
1. The note is being sustained over a system (note in standard notation is tied), or
2. The note is sustained, but a new articulation (such as a hammer-on, pull-off, slide or vibrato begins), or
3. The note is a barely audible "ghost" note (note in standard notation is also in parentheses).

# RECORDED VERSIONS
## The Best Note-For-Note Transcriptions Available

**RECORDED VERSIONS GUITAR ®**

**ALL BOOKS INCLUDE TABLATURE**